Headlines

rgell
gor

VIOLENCE

Molly Potter

A & C Black • London

INDIVIDUALS ENGAGING IN SOCIETY

Citizenship Foundation

Published 2010 by A & C Black Publishers Limited
36 Soho Square, London W1D 3QY
www.acblack.com

ISBN 978-1-4081-1354-7

Copyright text © Molly Potter 2010
Copyright illustrations © Karen Donnelly 2010
Series consultant: Roy Honeybone

The publishers are grateful for permission to reproduce the following:

p.60 The BBFC classification symbols © BBFC.   Every effort has been made to trace copyright
holders and obtain their permission for use of copyright material. The publishers would be pleased
to rectify any error or omission in future editions.

A CIP catalogue record for this book is available from the British Library.

Printed and bound in Great Britain by Caligraving.

A & C Black uses paper produced with elemental chlorine-free pulp, harvested from managed
sustainable forests.

Contents

Foreword

The books in this *Headlines* series tackle a range of important issues about which children and young people often think, especially when they hit the news headlines. Education for citizenship, though still non-statutory, should be an important element of the primary curriculum because it aims to help young people make sense of their world and understand the part they can play in making it a better place to live.

The Crick Report, in recommending that citizenship should become statutory in secondary schools, also suggested that it was relevant to primary children in helping them develop a sense of social and moral responsibility, understand their rights and responsibilities and also become politically literate. Critics might suggest that such aims are inappropriate for primary children but this is not so. Children from an early age actively attempt to make sense of the world around them in terms of important political ideas including fairness, power relations, laws and rules, right and wrong and so on. All of these are key citizenship concepts which, at secondary level focus on more explicitly political structures, but about which primary pupils are already developing ideas. In offering opportunities to debate and discuss what is happening in the world around them, and in helping young people develop their own ideas and their own voice, schools fulfil an important aim of general education which is no less than to help young people become responsible citizens.

Recently, the Independent Enquiry into Primary Education led by Sir Jim Rose, recommended that citizenship education, or social understanding, should be woven into a humanities strand, with history and geography, in order to remedy an important gap in the education provision of primary children. History and geography are important social strands of learning but in themselves, do not sufficiently address issues relating to the contemporary social world. Nor does it provide a curriculum space in which children can learn directly about their own rights and responsibilities, and develop the skills to think critically and thoughtfully about matters relating to their own welfare and that of wider society. Citizenship education also develops the skills of argument and debate so important in developing independence of thought and the confidence to know what one thinks and to express that appropriately in public settings. All these skills are developing rapidly during the primary years and citizenship education makes an important contribution to this process and that of developing respect for the views of others.

At about the same time that the Rose Review recommended citizenship should become an established strand of the curriculum, an authoritative study of primary education, led by Professor Robin Alexander, also recommended that citizenship education should be regarded as an essential part of primary education. One of the reasons the Cambridge Primary Review made this recommendation was because of citizenship's ability to nurture ethical reasoning. Moral education is a very necessary part of the education of every person, and yet very little direct attention is given to how schools help children develop a sense of right and wrong and work out for themselves what they think about issues in the wider world. Some teachers recoil at the notion that schools can or should get involved in telling children what their moral code should be. However, this is to misunderstand the purpose of enabling children to think ethically. In this sense moral instruction is not the same as moral education. Moral education nurtures children's ability to understand why some things in society are unacceptable, whilst other things are regarded as good, or important. Not that there will be complete agreement on such matters but that is not its purpose. Our society accepts that citizens' private moral views may differ and that different ways of life are acceptable so long as they do not operate to the detriment of others. That is why there is an important set of public values, which schools should convey to their pupils in class and reinforce through the practices and values of the institution, which are based on equality, respect for all, human rights, democracy and justice.

Schools, especially primary schools, are vital sites of social learning, where children, perhaps for the first time in their lives, begin to come up against people of different values and beliefs, behaviours, ethnicities, faiths, languages, countries of origins and so on. The primary socialisation that occurs within the family needs to be supplemented by secondary socialisation in which children learn there are other kinds of relation beyond those based on kinship and affection. However sound the education children gain at home, there are still important lessons to learn about the wider world and how it works and schooling plays a vital role in this. Moreover this is reinforced by the experiential citizenship learning which comes from everyday practices of involvement in school life, including student voice activities which provide practical experiences of community involvement, often beyond the school gates at local and even national and international levels. When messages from the taught and the experienced curriculum reinforce each other, children can become alerted to wider horizons and empowered to want to make a difference whether individually or with others.

The value of the Headlines series

This series of books addresses a range of issues about which primary school children are already aware and which they need to be able to understand, at an appropriate level. They are not trying to put 'old heads on young shoulders' or depress the children with the world's burdens. That would be wrong and unjustified. But the problems of violence, prejudice, poverty and war are issues which children can find deeply puzzling and we, as teachers, should try to help them deepen their understanding of them. There are several reasons for this.

The first is that children are often recipients of distorted messages which arrive through the medium of media headlines or sensationalising journalism. They may also be recipients of very one-sided views within the restricted family circle, so they lack the wider picture and do not develop the capacity to find out and think things through for themselves. They should also develop a sense of their own agency and appreciation of the fact that society is very much shaped by the individuals who make it up.

The material that has gone into this series is a mixture of knowledge and skills-based work which helps children to make sense of the issues and develop their conceptual understanding but also to develop essential thinking and emotional skills. Most of the material in this series is controversial in some way, some more than others. Naturally some of these topics are more challenging than others in content and different classes, even within the same school and year group, will vary in their capacity to deal with them adequately. So judicious choices may need to be made about which topics to cover and to what depth. Some of this material is perfectly suitable for use with children in Key Stage 3, given the wide variation in ability and experience within any age cohort of children.

Having emphasised the importance of developing children's thinking and empathy skills through discussing controversial issues, it needs to be emphasised that teachers may struggle to handle discussions of topics where their own knowledge is limited. It is important to let children air their views and to listen to the views of others but the role of the teacher is important in guiding the understanding of the children to deeper levels, in correcting important misinformation, and in balancing discussions when certain viewpoints are not spontaneously offered. Furthermore, discussing a social issue is not the same as discussing a scientific topic or the weather – it requires mastery of particular key words and ideas and particular forms of thinking and the skilled citizenship teacher provides structured opportunities for children to encounter these new ideas and use them in practice through debate, in group work, in presentations and in personal writing. That is why each book in this series provides a sound up-to-date introduction to the topic which, it is hoped teachers will find useful as background reading before teaching any of the lessons.

The Rose Review recommended that the stated aims of the primary curriculum should be the same as those now in place for the secondary curriculum, namely that it should enable students to become successful learners, confident individuals and responsible citizens. This surely makes practical sense. It cannot be helpful for our primary and secondary curricula to have different purposes because so much of what takes place in secondary schooling relies on the sound foundations laid in the primary school. In my own experience, primary teachers fully subscribe to the idea that the schooling they offer should help children prepare to play an active role as citizens, as laid out section 2 of the current PSHE and citizenship framework. However, teachers and schools differ in the extent to which they believe that social understanding and skills should be explicitly nurtured through the primary curriculum. The authors of this series firmly believe in the duty of the school to encourage the development of primary aged students as citizens, with rights and developing responsibilities, with social interests and skills. This is not to prematurely thrust them into adulthood but to help them become more rounded individuals better able to relate to others and better able to negotiate and contribute to the very complex world they inhabit.

Don Rowe
Director, Curriculum Development and Resources
Citizenship Foundation

Citizenship Foundation

is an educational charity which encourages and enables individuals to engage effectively in their communities and in democratic society at large. It works for better citizenship education, more effective participation in public life and stronger communities. Through curriculum development and support, the Foundation has championed the development of citizenship education in both primary and secondary schools, including its award-winning primary resources website 'Go Givers'. For more information about the Citizenship Foundation go to www.citizenshipfoundation.org.uk

INDIVIDUALS ENGAGING IN SOCIETY

Introduction

In a world where children are bombarded with violent images from screen media, there is considerable justification for exploration of this issue being routine in schools.

Children need first to have a basic understanding of what violence is, its effects, and that violence is generally understood to be unacceptable. Laws aim to protect people from violence and being a victim of violence is commonly agreed to be an infringement of human rights. In clarifying this, children might start to question why there is so much violence portrayed in screen media.

Media reports of violent crime

The images found in news reports of violent crime can be extremely disturbing and unsettling for children. On the other hand, due to the frequency of violent stories, adults can be desensitised to such images and forget that these crimes involve real victims and real suffering. Consequently, we can sometimes overlook the need to address any anxieties these images can cause in children.

Through news reports, children can receive a highly exaggerated impression of the prevalence and severity of violent crime. They need help to put such crimes into perspective. To do this they need to understand that:

- News programmes compete for viewing figures like any other programme. The fact that people tune in to watch bad – and not good – news means that graphic images appear frequently to keep the ratings higher.
- With communication links that mean news reporters can tap into a wealth of newsworthy material from around the world with incredible speed, the viewer receives a highly distilled version of worldwide violence. The images we receive bear little resemblance to the average walk around our local community.
- Violent crime statistics reveal that being directly involved in such crimes is still rare.

How does screen violence affect us?

With violent actions being commonplace in films, pop lyrics, TV programmes, computer games and websites, it is difficult to keep children completely protected from these images. For that reason there is a strong argument for helping children to develop a critical eye for such imagery, so they become equipped to cope with its prevalence.

Much research has been carried out to explore the effects of exposure to violence in screen media. Many theories have been investigated and many articles written on the topic, but no concrete evidence exists to say that watching screen violence is ever the single cause of an individual committing violent crime. It is not hard to conclude this yourself if you consider the many young people accessing screen violence that would certainly never commit a violent crime. This debate is a complex one and the following points outline some of the many stances people have taken on the issue.

- How violence in the media affects a person is highly individual. The effect will depend upon his or her attitudes, values, temperament and experiences.
- It might be that people with violent dispositions are more attracted to violence in screen media – rather than their viewing causing them to be violent.
- Most children have a good grasp of the interface between reality and fantasy and clearly understand that what they view would be totally unacceptable behaviour in reality.
- Watching violence might be cathartic for some individuals. In computer games some children get a feeling of completion, power and success that they might rarely feel elsewhere in their lives.
- The physiological effects of watching screen violence (adrenaline produced – raised heartbeat and stress) might cause children to play more energetically and aggressively.
- The violence portrayed is becoming more graphic and is appearing with greater frequency. This could be 'numbing' children to the effects of on-screen violence.
- Many adults are unaware of the journeys their children/pupils take into screen media. Age ratings for films may be less effective now that many children have access to the Internet and DVDs. Younger and younger children are being exposed to screen violence and this might result in more significant consequences.
- Some children play games using words taken directly from violent screen media, suggesting this may be affecting how they play.

Developing a critical eye for the violence children see in screen media

It does not look as though violence in screen media will become less pervasive in the future and it would be extremely hard to protect children from ever being exposed to violent images. This, therefore, spells out a need to provide children with a critical eye for the screen violence they do encounter. **Children need to move away from accepting that such images can wash over them without question.** They need to understand why such images are used and how unrealistic they can be. They also need to be certain of the boundary that must not be crossed in terms of screen violence and reality.

Children need to consider:

- The nature of violence in screen media can be very unrealistic: consequences are rarely shown – a violent act can be committed as if it is the only solution to a problem.
- In any film: Is the violence essential to the plot? Has it been included just for thrills? Does the violence have realistic consequences or does the plot just move on?
- There are different types of violence portrayed in screen media. Some might appear less 'serious' than others – for example, slapstick violence in a cartoon or 'funny' home videos might be seen as harmless violence for the sake of humour while real life shots of violence in a news story or a very violent scene in a film might be seen as very disturbing.
- Some violence might be seen as crucial to a film as it portrays the true horrors of historical events.
- Censorship of violence has been used in the past to prevent children from seeing on-screen violence. This might not be as effective as it once was because of Internet access, and some people believe it is up to individuals to decide what they do and don't watch. Many banned productions from the past have become classics in the present day.
- Many adults in children's lives are unaware of what their children are watching. Is this a good or a bad thing?

This book aims to help teachers:

- explore key issues on the topic of violence to develop pupils' understanding
- provide pupils with a realistic perspective on violent crime
- provide pupils with a critical eye for screen violence.

Key issues

Section 1
- to know what violence is.
- to consider language that is used to describe acts of violence.
- to consider their own and others' attitudes to violence.
- to understand that violence is generally considered to be 'wrong,' against the law, a violation of human rights and usually an inadequate solution to any problem.

- to consider violence in schools.
- to understand why violence happens.
- to understand the consequences of violence.
- to consider whether any violence is ever justified.
- to consider what self-defence is and when it is a legitimate course of action.
- to consider attitudes to and expectations of males and females behaviour with respect to violence.
- to consider how some people might find violence acceptable.
- to learn how anger management can sometimes prevent violence.

Section 2
- to clarify and understand what violent crime is.
- to explore pupils' perception of violent crime.
- to help pupils understand that the media's frequency and methods of reporting crime can give us an unrealistic idea of what is really happening.
- to develop a discerning eye for the way the media portrays violent crime.
- to consider appropriate safety advice for children.
- to be aware of what is being done to prevent crime and consider the effectiveness of some methods.

Section 3
- to explore pupils' perceptions of screen violence.
- to consider why so much violence is portrayed in screen media.
- to consider how watching violence might affect us.
- to develop a discerning eye for the violence portrayed in screen media.
- to consider the age classifications of films and whether they prevent young children from viewing violent material.

Please note: While violence is obviously a significant part of war and conflict, this book has only touched upon violence in these contexts because they will be covered more extensively in another book in the Headlines series: *War and Conflict*.

The CD-ROM

The CD-ROM provides extra resources for some lessons, such as newspaper reports, case studies or extra background information for pupils or teachers on topics discussed. Where this applies, these extra resources are listed in the lesson plan, and can be found organised by lesson on the CD-ROM. It also contains the activity sheets in the book as both PDF and Microsoft Word files. This allows them to be displayed on an electronic whiteboard, or be tailored by teachers to respond to a current event or issue. For more information on system requirements, please see the inside front cover.

Violence – the basics

This section aims to give pupils a basic understanding of violence and its related issues.

Key questions

- What is violence?
- Is violence wrong?
- Is any violence ever justified?
- What happens when people are violent?
- Why are people violent?
- Do we expect males to be more violent than females?
- Why is violence prevalent in entertainment?

Learning objectives of the activities

- to know what violence is.
- to consider language that is used to describe acts of violence.
- to consider their own and others' attitudes to violence.
- to understand that violence is generally considered to be 'wrong,' against the law, a violation of human rights and usually an inadequate solution to any problem.
- to consider violence in schools.
- to understand why violence happens.
- to understand the consequences of violence.
- to consider whether any violence is ever justified.
- to consider what self-defence is and when it is a legitimate course of action.
- to consider attitudes to and expectations of males and females behaviour with respect to violence.
- to consider how some people might find violence acceptable.
- to learn how anger management can sometimes prevent violence.

Learning objectives from the non-statutory guidance for PSHE and Citizenship

Pupils should be taught:

1 (a) to talk and write about their opinions, and explain their views, on issues that affect themselves and society

2 (b) why and how rules and laws are made and enforced, why different rules are needed in different situations and how to take part in making and changing rules

2 (c) to realise the consequences of anti-social and aggressive behaviours, such as bullying and racism, on individuals and communities

2 (f) to resolve differences by looking at alternatives, making decisions and explaining choices

4 (a) that their actions affect themselves and others, to care about other people's feelings and to try to see things from their points of view

4 (e) to recognise and challenge stereotypes

SPEAKING AND LISTENING

Listening
Pupils should be taught to:

2a. identify the gist of an account or key points in a discussion and evaluate what they hear

2b. ask relevant questions to clarify, extend and follow up ideas

2e. respond to others appropriately, taking into account what they say

Group discussion and interaction
Pupils should be taught to:

3a. make contributions relevant to the topic and take turns in discussion

3c. qualify or justify what they think after listening to others' questions or accounts

3d. deal politely with opposing points of view and enable discussion to move on

Drama
4a. create, adapt and sustain different roles, individually and in groups

READING

Understanding texts
Pupils should be taught to:

2a. use inference and deduction

Reading for information
Pupils should be taught to:

3c. obtain specific information through detailed reading

3g. consider an argument critically

Non-fiction and non-literary texts
Pupils should be taught to:

5g. engage with challenging and demanding subject matter.

WRITING

Composition
Pupils should be taught to:

1a. choose form and content to suit a particular purpose [for example, notes to read or organise thinking, plans for action, poetry for pleasure]

1b. broaden their vocabulary and use it in inventive ways

1c. use language and style that are appropriate to the reader

1d. use features of layout, presentation and organisation effectively

Planning and drafting
Pupils should be taught to:

2a. plan – note and develop initial ideas

2b. draft – develop ideas from the plan into structured written text

Key Vocabulary
- violence
- unacceptable
- self-defence
- managing anger

ACTIVITY 1

What is most violent?

Type of activity:
Diamond nine

Learning objective:
to consider degrees of violence.

Resources:
Pupil activity sheet 1 'What is most violent?' (p20); one per pair

What to do:

1 Give pupils a copy of the sheet 'What is most violent?' (p20)

2 Ask pairs of pupils to order the nine smaller diamonds into a larger diamond shape with the action they believe to be most violent at the top and then the next two most violent actions just below the most important point…and so on…to the action they consider is least violent at the bottom.

3 Ask pupils to discuss the following question:

"what makes an action seem very violent?"

4 Take feedback from the whole class and discuss

Key points:

• The degree of which a particular action might seem more or less violent might depend upon the degree of injury, the intention, whether it's legal or not, how 'controlled' the violence is, whether a weapon has been used etc.

Support/extension:

• Pupils could list some other examples of violence and position them on an imaginary scale from not violent to extremely violent. Pupils could also perform this activity with the newspaper articles from Lesson 10 'A closer look at self-defence' found on the CD-ROM.

ACTIVITY 2

Words for violence

Type of activity:
Investigation

Learning objective:
to consider the language used to describe acts of violence, to further consolidate what violence is.

What to do:

1 Ask pairs of pupils to list as many verbs as they can (with the help of a dictionary and/or thesaurus) that could be an act of violence (e.g., hit, punch, injure, fight, stab, swipe, poke, wound, bash, scratch, thump, beat, cut).

2 Display the following questions and ask pupils to discuss them in pairs:
• Why do you think there are so many words to describe violent acts?
• How do these words make you feel?
• What do these words make you think of?

3 Ask pairs to volunteer any points their discussions covered.

Key points:

• There are probably many words to describe violent acts because we have a very rich language that has been added to by many different invaders throughout history (Angles, Saxons, Jutes, Vikings, Normans). These invaders (and others) will have exhibited violent behaviour. Although violence has changed its nature throughout history (weapons have changed for example), it has been present throughout recorded history.

• Pupils will come up with a range of feelings and thoughts prompted by these words – from fear to anger. Reassure pupils that all of these feelings are normal. Violence is a topic that can result in strong emotions.

• Ask pupils to record what these words make them think of – in pictorial or written form. At the end of a series of activities on violence, you could ask pupils if their view of violence has changed in any way or if they can explain why they think they got the images they did.

- Pupils could try and draw an abstract picture that, for them, represents violence and write the emotions that violence might make a person feel.

Different attitudes to violence

Type of activity:
Agreement spectrum

Learning objective:
to explore different attitudes towards violence.

Resources:
Pupil activity sheet 2 'Different attitudes to violence' (p21); one per pupil

What to do:

1 Give individual pupils a copy of the sheet 'Different attitudes to violence' (p21) and demonstrate how the agreement spectrum works. Explain that if you placed the cross in the middle of the line, it would mean you neither agreed nor disagreed.

2 Ask individual pupils to complete the sheet.

3 Next ask pupils to work in pairs and discuss why they have placed each cross where they have. As with all agreement spectrums, the value is in the discussions they initiate.

4 As a whole class, complete the session by asking pupils to volunteer any thoughts they have developed about violence. You could use the activity sheets and the key points below to help guide any discussion.

Key points:

- Some people (pacifists) do believe violence is always wrong; therefore retaliation in their eyes is just as wrong as initiating violence. Most people do consider most violence to be wrong but consider that violence in war, policing against violence or in self-defence is not wrong. Other people might not ever have questioned whether violence is wrong or not. If a person has experienced or witnessed violence in their life, they might believe it is 'normal' behaviour for sorting out difficult situations and not know it is actually wrong.
- Violence is usually punished in schools. This is meant to act as a deterrent for further violence and openly show other pupils that violence is unacceptable.
- Some people use violence because they cannot work out another way of solving a problem or because they cannot express complicated emotions. In most situations where violence is used, there is usually a much better solution and it usually involves learning different behaviour. For example, if a person is violent when someone makes them angry, they could learn to take time out, cool down and then communicate with the person that made them angry – to work out a solution.
- People are not always obviously angry when they commit violence. They sometimes do it to look tough or because they want to impress others, for example.
- Empathy – the ability to understand how another person is feeling – can prevent violence.

Support/extension:

- Pupils could discuss what they believe is appropriate punishment for violence in schools and/or discuss what they think would be the best way to prevent a pupil that had used violence from using it again.
- Pupils could investigate the use of corporal punishment throughout history (either by research or interviewing adults) and discuss whether or not they believe it was an appropriate way to punish children.

Violence – rules, laws and human rights

Type of activity:
Investigation

Learning objective:
to understand that nearly all violence is considered to be wrong in the eyes of the law, human rights and school rules.

Resources:
Pupil activity sheet 3 'Violence – rules, laws and human rights' (p22); one per pair

What to do:

1 Give pairs of pupils a copy of the sheet 'Violence – rules, laws and human rights' (p22) and read through it as a whole class. Question pupils to check their understanding – particularly in the sample of UN human rights. Explain that the United Nations Declaration of Human Rights is a list of rights that the UN believes everyone is entitled to and many countries worldwide value, honour and have signed up to these rights. The full list can be found on the CD-ROM.

2 Ask pairs of pupils to write down or underline all the evidence that they can find on this sheet that implies violence should not happen and/or that people should be protected from violence.

3 Ask the whole class to feed back the evidence they found and explain what it shows/implies. For example:
- *'We will treat everyone as we would like to be treated.'* People would not want to be treated with violence.
- *'One of the main jobs of the law is to control and prevent violence.'* This implies that violence is something that people should be protected from.
- *'should act towards one another in a spirit of goodwill.'* Acting in the spirit of goodwill would not include violence.
- *'to be safe.'* People do not feel safe when they are a victim of violence.

Key points:

- Except in a few circumstances (e.g. self-defence, war, police trying to uphold the law), in the UK violence is considered to be wrong and against the law.
- In schools, punishments are usually issued when staff learn that a pupil has been violent and in society people are arrested, tried and issued punishments when they commit violence because it is against the law.
- It does not seem to be a tall order to expect that every person can live a life that is free from violence and that is why it is considered to be a basic human right.

Support/extension:

- Using the activity sheet, less able pupils could find the evidence in the first two boxes only and have those in the third box underlined for them.
- Pupils could write in their own words the reason why they think violence is wrong.
- A visit from a police officer could be arranged so that he or she could talk about appropriate use of force in dealing with crime.

Violence in school

Type of activity:
Questionnaire design

Learning objective:
to investigate pupil's opinions about violence in school, and consider what happens in school to deal with violence.

Resources:
Pupil activity sheet 4 'Violence in school' (p23); one per pair

What to do:

1 Give pairs of pupils a copy of the sheet 'Violence in school' (p23) and explain that in their pairs, they are going to create a questionnaire that will be used to investigate pupils' opinions about violence. Explain that the sheet includes some ideas to start them off.

2 Encourage pupils to think carefully about the questions they are going to include and what the answers will tell them.

3 Once pupils have completed their questionnaires, they could:
- ask fellow classmates to complete them
- send one or two to be completed collectively by different classes in the school
- ask individual pupils from throughout the school to complete them during break time or another suitable time in the day.

4 Once the questionnaires have been filled in, pupils could report back to the whole class:
• something they found interesting or unexpected in the answers they got back
• an answer they expected – and got!

Alternatively: these issues could be investigated by the school council and their findings reported to the whole school.

Key points:

• It is generally deemed appropriate that absolutely no violence happens in schools – even in retaliation. Most schools put effort into preventing and dealing with violence.
• A school is legally bound to outline its procedure for dealing with bullying (violent or not) either in an anti-bullying policy or as part of a behaviour policy.

Support/extension:

• Less able pupils could work in mixed-ability pairs.
• Pupils could design an anti-violence logo for the school.
• More able pupils could devise a questionnaire for teachers.
• More able pupils could investigate the school's policies for evidence of anti-violence.
• Pupils could develop a survey to find out a greater number of pupils' opinions (e.g. is violence always wrong? Yes/No, Suitable punishment for one pupil hitting another pupil is: lose a break time, a letter home to parents/carer, a discussion with the headteacher about what happened, etc. They could also display their findings.
• Pupils could draw a 'safety map' of the school that highlights places in the school that they might feel at risk from bullying or violence. They could colour code their map for areas in the school where they feel safe, unsafe or neither. This could open up discussions as to what could be done to make the unsafe areas feel more safe.

ACTIVITY 6

The consequences of violence

Type of activity:
Discussion

Learning objective:
to consider that the consequences of violence in school are never positive and how violence can be avoided.

Resources:
Pupil activity sheet 5 'The consequences of violence' (p24); one per pair

What to do:

1 Give pairs of pupils a copy of the sheet 'The consequences of violence' (p24) and read through it. Ask pairs of pupils to develop a realistic ending for each scenario – being mindful of the given consequence in the first column.

2 Ask a few pairs to share their endings with the whole class. Point out any endings that are unrealistic (e.g. computer-game style blood and gore). As a class agree on one likely ending for each scenario and write it in note form for all to see.

3 Then ask pairs of pupils to discuss questions 1 and 2.
  1 Does violence ever seem like a good way to sort something out?
  Pupils might conclude that there is almost always a better solution than violence.
  2 What needed to happen to stop the violence in each of these situations?
  • People should not have made nasty comments.
  • When someone recognised they had become angry, they could have taken time out to calm down. Then they would be more likely to be able to sort out the situation without becoming violent.
  • An adult might have been able to help with the situation.
  • Feelings needed to be communicated and apologies given.

This issue of avoiding violence and managing anger is explored further in the activity: What might stop a person from being violent? (p24)

4 Return to a whole class discussion to consider the key points that arise from questions 1 and 2.

Key points:

- The consequences of violence are nearly always very negative and on the whole, can make a situation much worse than if violence had not been resorted to.
- Retaliation might seem like a good idea sometimes but the response of the other person is unpredictable and you cannot assume things won't just escalate.
- People cannot help getting angry but they can decide how to behave as a result of that anger. If people learn to take time out and 'cool off' (either using calming thoughts or 'punching a pillow' type methods) before dealing with someone that has made them

angry, they are much less likely to use violence towards that person.
- In most of the situations on the activity sheet, 'good' or assertive communication could have prevented the violence. For example, Tom could have said to Ash, "You might think I am stupid, but I don't."

Support/extension:

- Less able pupils could draw their story endings using stick people.
- Pupils could decide on and then role-play a more effective ending to the first part of each scenario (the part written in bold).
- Pupils could devise some top tips for avoiding violence.

ACTIVITY 7

Why are people violent?

Type of activity:
Sorting activity to prompt discussion

Learning objective:
to consider the reasons why people are violent and whether these reasons ever make the violence right.

Resources:
Pupil activity sheet 6 'Why are people violent?' (p25); one per group

What to do:

1 Give groups of pupils a copy of the sheet 'Why are people violent?' (p25) and read through the information as a class.

2 With pupils working in mixed ability groups of about four, ask them to number the actions in order from the most to the least 'wrong'. They could score the least wrong as '7' down to the most wrong as '1'. This helps pupils to consider each scenario. Their scoring will probably depend upon the following factors:
- the level of provocation
- any imbalance of power
- the vulnerability of the victim
- the nature/severity of the violence
- how much in control of their actions the violent person appears to be
- age/ability to understand that violence is wrong.

3 Next ask groups of pupils to consider the reasons why each person has been violent. Do any of these reasons seem more acceptable than others?

4 Ask groups to try and work out what they think needs to happen in each scenario on the sheet to prevent the person from being violent. Ask each group to feedback one 'preventing violence' suggestion to the whole class and list them for all to see.

Key points:

- People are violent for a variety of reasons. However, whatever reason a person may have, violence is very rarely the right thing to do, or the best solution. In law, violence is only ever considered justified if it is done in self-defence. This means that:

1 the violence is directed only against someone who is attacking
2 the aim of the violence is only to stop the attack
3 the violence done in self-defence is the only way the attack can be stopped.
Number 3 would imply that retaliation (e.g. after a person has been hit) is

not always the right thing to do in a school setting – as there is usually the alternative option of telling an adult. This can be discussed.

- People can be violent because they have no other way of showing their emotions, they are frustrated, trying to impress, drunk, etc.

Support/extension:

- Less able pupils could cut out each row of the table so that they can physically move them to order them.
- Pupils could write an agony-aunt style letter that gives anti-violence advice to one of the people on the sheet.

Seeing violence as acceptable

Type of activity:
Graffiti page

Learning objective:
to consider how violence could become acceptable or glamorous to a young person.

Resources:
Large sheet of paper with outline of a person drawn in centre; one per group

What to do:

1 Remind pupils that violence (with a few exceptions) is considered to be wrong.

2 Hand out large sheets of paper with the outline of a person drawn in the centre – one for each group of about six pupils. Explain that the character in the centre of the page does not believe violence is wrong and in fact s/he thinks it's just part of life. Ask smaller groups or pairs of pupils to write the reasons why the person might believe this.

3 Discuss the pupils' ideas and collate these on a clean copy of the sheet so they can be displayed.

Key points:

- Below are some reasons a young person might have for believing violence isn't bad.

  1 It is what many of their peers are doing.

  2 They have become hardened to violence and no longer empathise with the victim.

  3 They believe violence is in some way glamorous and exciting.

  4 They have seen a lot of violence.

  5 No one has ever helped this person understand that violence is wrong.

  6 They do not know the difference between violence in screen media and reality.

  7 They have been a victim of violent acts.

  8 They have been lead to believe that carrying a weapon is cool and has some kudos.

Support/extension:

- Pupils could discuss how such a person's viewpoint about violence could be changed.

Is violence always wrong?

Type of activity:
Looking at storyboards to prompt discussion

Learning objective:
to consider situations when violence might possibly be justified.

Resources:
Pupil activity sheet 7 'Is violence always wrong?' (p26) and Pupil activity sheet 8 'Is violence always wrong? Questions for discussion' (p27); one of each per pair

What to do:

1 Give pairs of pupils a copy of the sheet 'Is violence always wrong?' (p26). Look at the first storyboard and ask pupils to discuss the questions about scenario 1, found on the sheet 'Is violence always wrong? Questions for discussion' (p27).

2 Bring the whole class together and discuss the pupils' answers.

3 Next ask pupils to consider the second and third scenarios on the sheet and answer the questions in pairs. Take feedback for each scenario.

4 Ask the class whether they think any of the violence in these stories is OK and if so why? Use the key points below to help with the discussion.

Key points:

- In scenario 1 Darrel uses violence in self-defence. In the eyes of the law, his violence would not be seen as a crime because he used it a) only against the person that was attacking him, b) his intention was only to stop the violence and escape, and c) because the person grabbed him from behind, there probably was not another way of preventing the attack.
- In scenario 2 the policewoman used force to stop the violent criminal but only after she had shouted a warning that the robber ignored. The police have very strict guidelines about when they can use violence and would get into trouble if they did not follow them.
- In scenario 3 we are assuming that the two sets of soldiers are fighting because their countries are at war. Some people believe that war is never justified but when two countries are at war, soldiers fighting soldiers is considered to be appropriate and legal action. Even wars have guidelines about how they should be fought but not every country follows these. Wars start for a variety of reasons, e.g. threat of terrorist attack, friction between different races or nationalities over land, but war is not usually entered into without provocation (even if sometimes this is just perceived and not real). The UN might say that war could sometimes be viewed as large scale self-defence against an attacking. However, every war causes much debate over why it happened and how it could have been avoided.

Support/extension:

- Pupils could discuss why kicking a person who has kicked you at school is not necessarily self- defence. (There is another course of action open to you).

A closer look at self-defence

Type of activity:
Considering a newspaper story

Learning objective:
to consider what self-defence is and when it is a legitimate course of action.

Resources:
Pupil activity sheet 9 'A closer look at self-defence' (p28); one per pair

What to do:

Note: Newspapers are a valuable resource for researching and investigating violence. The pupils could be encouraged to collect their own 'latest' stories from local papers. You (the teacher) could also collect articles that could be used with your class to explore issues relating to violence and self-defence. Some examples can be found on the CD-ROM.

1 Give pairs of pupils a copy of the sheet 'A closer look at self-defence' (p28) and discuss the legal definition of self-defence at the top of the sheet. Check pupils' understanding by asking if each of the bullet-pointed examples would be considered self-defence or not. For each example, you could ask the three questions:

a) is the violence only against the person who is attacking?

b) is the aim of the violence only to stop the attack?

c) is violence the only way the attack can be stopped?

- A man used a baseball bat to threaten someone who was playing loud music in the house next door. (Not self-defence)
- A shopkeeper threw a tin can at a robber who was pointing a gun at him. (Self-defence)
- An adult hit a child because the child had vandalised their garden. (Not self-defence)
- Yaz and Julie never get on and often argue. Yaz punched Julie as they were walking into school. Julie didn't do anything until breaktime when she kicked Yaz. (Not strictly speaking self-defence as Julie did not kick Yaz to prevent the violence.)

2 Read though the newspaper story – explain what some of the more difficult words mean to ensure all pupils understand the article.

3 Ask pairs of pupils to underline anything that suggests Mr Sowerby was acting in self-defence in one colour and anything that suggests he was not acting in self-defence in another colour. Pupils do not need to record their reasons for including each detail as long as they can verbally justify the position of each piece of evidence. Some examples:

Anything that suggests it was self-defence	Anything that suggests it was not self-defence
<ul><li>he was trying to avoid a fight with Stephen Walsh</li><li>did not intend to seriously injure or kill the deceased</li><li>he was defending himself.</li></ul>	<ul><li>injuries which eventually killed him.</li><li>(implies excessive violence was used – more than was needed to stop the situation)</li><li>Sowerby should have walked away from the argument.</li><li>he pushed him through the French windows of the Saracen's Head pub (possibly excessive action for preventing violence)</li><li>his actions were unnecessarily aggressive and had a real risk of hurting Mr Walsh.</li></ul>

4 At the end, ask pupils to scribble on a piece of scrap people either that the story is one of 'self-defence' or 'not self-defence' and the reason for their final decision.

5 If you have a reasonable split, you could ask pupils to debate this issue further. They can use the reasons they scribbled on the scrap paper to help support their argument. Otherwise, take a tally of the pupils' conclusions and declare the result.

Key points:

- Some people use self-defence as an excuse to be violent.
- Alcohol can impact on a person's judgement and level of aggression.
- The law states clearly what self-defence is, but sometimes a court case (with a jury) is needed to finally decide if an action was self-defence or not. This

in effect is what the class has done – been a 'jury'.

Support/extension:

- Less able pupils could just consider the text written in bold.
- Pupils could consider questions they would like to ask Mr Sowerby if they could – to help them work out the truth.

ACTIVITY 11

Violence: male or female?

Type of activity:
Picture interpretation leading to discussion

Learning objective:
to explore gender stereotypes in violence.

Resources:
Pupil activity sheet 10 'Violence: male or female?' (p29); one per pupil

What to do:

1 Ask pupils to look at the sheet 'Violence: Male or Female?' (p29) and individually decide the gender of each of the labelled people. Encourage pupils to be realistic and honest and really consider whether it seems as if it could be a male or a female. Some pupils might deliberately demonstrate that they do not do gender stereotyping. Do not worry if this is the case as the issues can still be discussed.

2 For each labelled person, ask some pupils what sex they made 'it' and why.

3 Discuss the findings. Ask pupils:
- Do you think violence is seen as more of a male thing than a female thing? (People usually do, although recent media coverage of the increases in female violence might have changed this view. Furthermore, as a female being violent seems more shocking than male violence, it can leave a stronger and longer lasting impression.)
- If a female is violent, do you think people are more shocked than if a male is violent? (Usually – as it goes expect what is conditioned female behaviour.)
- In what ways might people expect boys to be violent? (Boys are encouraged to be more physical in their play, e.g., they might be bought guns and swords to play with.)
- Are all boys violent? (No!) Are all girls not violent? (No!) These are stereotypes. Stereotypes can be harmful because people can feel they need to stick to them and be teased if they deviate from them.
- Martial arts are about control. Do you think females do martial arts as much as males? (If so, it might be because martial arts are about control and not about aggression.)
- In the light of the fact that aggression and violence can cause a lot of suffering and are rarely the best way to solve a problem, what messages do you think all children (male and female) should receive about violence?

Key points:

- There has always been a nature versus nurture discussion about male violence. Some people say males are instinctively more violent, others say it is learnt behaviour and could be unlearnt.
- Violent crime committed by females is increasing, but both convictions and victims of criminal crime are still significantly more frequent. According to police records (2007/8) 87% of violent incidents involve male offenders.
- When a female commits a violent crime it receives more media attention than when a male commits the same crime.

In history women were put into asylums for committing violent crimes, when men were sent to prison for the same crime. This is because violence in women is seen as far more of a deviation from expectations than when men are violent.

Support/extension:

- Pupils could look at toys that are traditionally aimed at boys and those aimed at girls and consider what the toys might encourage the different sexes to do. For example: Girls; nurture, clean, look after things, be patient. Boys; be physical, fight.

Type of activity:
Discussion and role play

Learning objective:
to learn how anger management can sometimes prevent violence.

Resources:
Pupil activity sheet 11 'What might stop a person from being violent?' (p30) and Pupil activity sheet 12 'Sam's story. Questions for discussion' (p31); one each per pair

What might stop a person from being violent?

What to do:

1 Give pairs of pupils a copy of the sheet, 'What might stop a person from being violent?'(p30) and read through section A. (Notice that Sam could be a boy or a girl. This has been done so as not to stereotype this behaviour as male. Pupils can choose whether their Sam is a girl or a boy.)

2 Ask pairs of pupils to talk about what they think will happen after Sam has hit Ali. It is unlikely to be a 'happy ending'. Discuss how violence is usually the worst possible way of responding to a situation.

3 Next, as a whole class, read through section B. Explain that Sam received this support because his/her teachers were worried about his/her tendency to become violent so quickly. As a class you could discuss how each of the things Sam learnt could be effective in preventing him/her from hitting someone.

4 Ask pairs of pupils to discuss the questions on the sheet, 'Sam's story: Questions for discussion' (p31) and then ask the whole class to feedback their thoughts. Some guidance for each question is as follows.

    1 heart beat gets faster   breathes more quickly   face goes red
gritted teeth   fists clenched   forehead wrinkles   body gets tense
shaking
Some children do need help to recognise these symptoms of anger so that they are aware they need to calm down.

    2 Calming: breathing deeply and counting to ten, making him/herself think about something positive. Using up energy: punching the air, running fast.

    3 The anger will make it unlikely that s/he will be able to sort anything out because it makes it more likely that Ali will get upset and that the situation will escalate.

    4 Sam needs his/her ball returned.

    5 Find an adult that will go and fetch the ball (if s/he asks nicely!)

    6 a Sam is likely to feel more angry if Ali kicked the ball over the fence deliberately. It will also make the anger targeted at Ali. If Ali did not kick it over deliberately, Sam might just feel angry about the fact s/he no longer has his/her ball. If Sam can work out what s/he is actually angry about, it will make it easier for him/her to communicate what s/he needs, which in turn will make him/her less likely to get angry.

    b No, the ball still needs to be fetched.

5 Now ask pairs of pupils to complete the role play in section C of the sheet 'What might stop a person from being violent?' (p30). Ask willing pairs to demonstrate what they have worked out to the whole class. Point out how and why these endings are preferable to Sam using violence.

Key points:

- Anger management can help prevent violence.
- It takes practice to get good at managing anger.
- When a person gets angry, they do have a choice about how they behave as a result of that anger.
- Thinking logically about the solution to a problem and focussing on what needs to happen to sort it out is better than responding aggressively.

Support/extension:

- Less able pupils could illustrate the answers to questions 1 and 2.
- Pupils could write or draw a guide to 'preventing violence caused by anger'.

What is most violent?

Here are some actions that may be considered violent.
Cut out the diamonds.
Re-order them into a larger diamond shape. Put the most violent action at the top and the least violent action at the bottom.
Discuss why you have chosen this order.

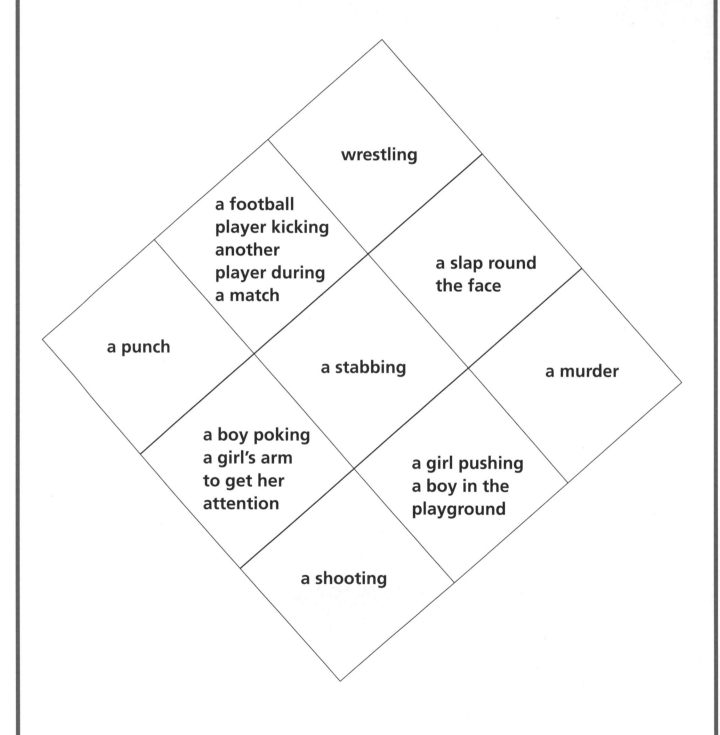

wrestling

a football player kicking another player during a match

a slap round the face

a punch

a stabbing

a murder

a boy poking a girl's arm to get her attention

a girl pushing a boy in the playground

a shooting

Different attitudes to violence

On these lines, put a cross (X) to show how much you agree or disagree with each statement.

I think violence is always wrong.

strongly disagree _____ strongly agree

If someone hits you, I think it is OK to hit them back.

strongly disagree _____ strongly agree

Violence in school should always be punished.

strongly disagree _____ strongly agree

I think some people use violence because they do not know another way of sorting out a problem.

strongly disagree _____ strongly agree

I think violence only happens when a person is angry.

strongly disagree _____ strongly agree

If you are violent towards another person it means that you stop seeing them as a person who can be hurt.

strongly disagree _____ strongly agree

I think a violent person can learn not to be violent.

strongly disagree _____ strongly agree

I hate it when people are violent.

strongly disagree _____ strongly agree

Violence – rules, laws and human rights

Some school rules

- We will treat everyone as we would like to be treated.
- We will look after school property.
- We will never accept bullying of any kind and will always report any bullying that we see.

Violence and the law

One of the main jobs of the law is to control and prevent violence.

Use of force that is not committed by the police, the *armed forces* or done in self-defence is against the law and is therefore a crime.

A violent crime is where someone uses or threatens to use violence upon a victim. This includes crimes with or without weapons.

United Nations Declaration of Human Rights

Article 1
All human beings are born free and equal in *dignity* and *rights*. They have been given reason and a *conscience* and should act towards one another in a spirit of *goodwill*.

Article 3
Everyone has the right to life, freedom and to be safe.

Article 5
No one shall be tortured or be treated or punished in a cruel, *inhuman* or *degrading* way.

Part of Article 14
Everyone has the right to seek and to enjoy *asylum* from *persecution* in other countries.

Part of Article 29
In *exercising* their rights and freedoms, everyone shall be limited only by law and by the respect for the rights and freedoms of others.

Word meanings

armed forces: the military (the army, the RAF or the navy).

dignity: a sense of self respect and pride. If you are treated with dignity – you are respected.

right: something that you are entitled to.

conscience: the part of a person that tells them what is right or wrong.

goodwill: friendliness and a willingness to help others.

degrading: particularly horrible, humiliating and showing no respect

asylum: a place of safety

persecution: being picked on and bullied
exercising: doing or carrying out

Violence in school

With a partner, you are going to write a questionnaire about violence. The questions you ask should help you to investigate what pupils in your school think about violence. The ideas on this sheet are to help you.

Finding out opinions
Do pupils think that violence in school is always wrong?

- If someone hit you on the playground, what would you do?
- Is hitting ever OK?
- Is nudging ever OK?

Investigating what pupils know
What is done to try and stop violence from happening in school?

- What rules do pupils know about that make it clear violence is not allowed?
- What do pupils think teachers do to prevent violence from happening?

Investigating what pupils know
Where and when is violence most likely to happen if it does happen?

- Are there times in the school day when violence is more likely to happen?
- Are there any places where pupils feel unsafe in school because of the threat of violence?

Investigating what pupils know
What punishments do pupils think are appropriate if one child hit another?

- Do all teachers give the same punishment?
- Are punishments the only thing that happens after a person has been hit?

Finding out opinions
Do pupils think corporal punishment in school used to work?

- Have pupils heard any stories about corporal punishment from their parents or grandparents?
- Do pupils think that using violence to punish violence works?

The consequences of violence

Work with a partner.

Make up a realistic ending for each of these stories.

Consequence	What happened
The situation gets out of hand	**Ash said Tom was stupid**, so Tom hit Ash. Ash then kicked Tom so Tom punched Ash and . . . _____ _____
Makes someone feel awful	**Mo was extremely pleased with himself because he had managed to make a really impressive model of a robot. Kamil was annoyed because Mo had used all the materials he had brought into school to make the robot**, so he shoved Mo and . . . _____ _____
Injury	**Louise said Delyth was 'really nasty' for not letting her use her sharpener. This made Delyth annoyed** and she threw a metal sharpener at Louise. The sharpener caught Louise in the eye. This made Louise's eye . . . _____ _____
Nothing gets sorted out	**Katy and Aisha both wanted to use the one plastic hoop on the playground. Katy grabbed it at the same time as Aisha** and both pulled on the hoop, each insisting that they were going to play with it . . . _____ _____
Punishment	**Dipak said Charlie was rubbish at football.** Charlie kicked Dipak at breaktime. The teacher on playground duty saw this happen . . . _____ _____

Now discuss these questions with your partner.

1 Does violence ever seem like a good way to sort something out?

2 What needed to happen to stop the violence in each of these situations?

Why are people violent?

Which action is the most unacceptable? Number these actions from the most wrong (1) to the least wrong (7).

Person	Reason	What they did	Score
Anu aged 6	When Anu gets angry, she is often violent.	Anu got angry about not getting the part she wanted in the school play and punched Josie.	
Georgie aged 8	Georgie has seen a lot of violence in her life and believes it is the best way to sort something out.	Georgie kicked Shirin because she wouldn't let her have one of her crisps at playtime.	
Pablo aged 11	Pablo believes that if someone hurts you, you have the right to hurt them back.	Pablo shoved Frankie because Frankie had deliberately tripped him up. They are both in the same class and usually get on well together.	
Yasmin aged 14	Yasmin gets a thrill out of doing things that could get her into trouble.	Yasmin threw a stone at an old lady.	
Clive aged 15	Clive belongs to a gang and in that gang everyone is expected to be violent to prove themselves.	Clive slapped Ali – who is 11 – in front of some of his gang members.	
Trisha aged 16	Trisha thinks it's important to look tough so people respect you.	Trisha pushed Don – who is 16 – because all her friends were watching and she wanted to look tough.	
Boz aged 18	Boz often gets drunk and finds that it makes him behave differently. Usually he gets more aggressive.	Boz hit a stranger in the street. The stranger was male and about the same age as Boz.	

Is violence always wrong?

Scenario 1

| When Darrel was walking along the street, he was grabbed round the neck by a person from behind. | Darrel panicked but managed to use his elbow to dig into the sides of whoever was grabbing him. | The person who had grabbed Darrel was winded and Darrel managed to escape. |

Scenario 2

| A robber armed with a baseball bat entered a shop. The robber used the bat to smash part of a window display. | The robber threatened to hit the shopkeeper with the bat if he did not hand over all the money. | As the robber left the shop, a policewoman shouted at the robber to stop but when the robber ignored her command, she used force to wrestle the robber to the ground. |

Scenario 3

| Some soldiers with guns are hiding in an empty building. | From a window they spot some enemy soldiers running towards them. | They aim at the enemy soldiers and open fire. |

8 Is violence always wrong? Questions for discussion

Discuss these questions with a partner.

Scenario 1

- In what way was Darrel violent?
- Do you think Darrel was right to be violent and if so why?
- What did Darrel's violence enable him to do?

Notes

Scenario 2

- In what way was the robber violent?
- What did the policewoman do before she used force?
- For what reasons did the policewoman use force? (to stop the robber and prevent herself and others from getting hurt)

Notes

Scenario 3

- What did the soldiers do that was violent?
- Who were they violent towards?
- Why do you think the soldiers are shooting at each other?

Notes

A closer look at self-defence

Self-defence is where violence is used to stop a person who is trying to hurt you. The law is very clear about what self-defence is. It says that an act of violence is self-defence if:

1 The violence is only against the person who is attacking.
2 The aim of the violence is only to stop the attack.
3 It is the only way the attack can be stopped.

Do you think this is a story of self-defence?

"I attacked in self-defence," Devon manslaughter jury told

Wednesday, September 03, 2008, 23:00
Exeter Express and Echo

A MAN has told a jury he acted in self-defence when he pushed another pubgoer, causing severe injuries which eventually killed him.

Glenn Sowerby, 45, yesterday said that he was trying to avoid a fight with Stephen Walsh when he pushed him through the French windows of the Saracen's Head pub in Fairfield Terrace, Newton Abbot.

Mr Walsh, 51, hit his head on the ground outside the pub as he fell backwards, suffering a fractured skull and internal bleeding to his brain.

The court has heard he spent months in hospital, was moved to a care home suffering from total paralysis and died on September 17 last year from broncho-pneumonia after his condition became worse.

Sowerby, of Oakland Road, Newton Abbot, has denied a charge of manslaughter.

It is the prosecution's case that Sowerby did not intend to seriously injure or kill the deceased but that his actions were unnecessarily aggressive and had a real risk of hurting Mr Walsh. It is the defence's case that he was defending himself.

Sowerby denied losing his temper and aggressively pushing Mr Walsh, when he gave evidence over the incident at the pub, which happened on Sunday, May 13, last year.

Prosecutor Jonathan Barnes, cross-examining, suggested Sowerby should have walked away from the argument.

"There was no way I was walking away because he was nose to nose with me and I was in a confined space," said Sowerby. "The man wanted me outside. What do I know, if I'd turned my back on him, he wouldn't have hit me?"

He added: "I had stood back and he was following me, he had his nose to nose with me. He's come back to confront me again."

The prosecutor suggested Sowerby should have said, "look Steve, I don't want any trouble."

The defendant said this was impractical, as he feared that Mr Walsh was going to attack him and he had to push him away before that happened.

Sowerby disagreed with the prosecutor that the reason he then followed the deceased out into the garden was because he wanted to have a fight.

Pubgoer Kevin Joint had earlier given evidence about how he had been out drinking with Sowerby that day.

Mr Joint said he was sitting in the pub garden with his dog when he saw Mr Walsh fall backwards.

He agreed with defence counsel Martin Edmunds that Sowerby had then come outside and said: "What have I done?"

Mr Edmunds said: "The way he said it was as if he was confused?"

The witness replied: "Yes."

The witness said they were both upset after the incident and had gone to another pub for a drink. He said he did not actually see what caused Mr Walsh to fall through the French windows.

The trial continues.

Violence: male or female?

Decide whether you think each person in the pictures below is male or female and then label them. There are both males and females on this sheet.

SHEET 11: What might stop a person from being violent?

A) Sometimes people are violent because they are angry.

Sam has a really short fuse. This means Sam gets angry really easily. When Sam gets angry, s/he often hits someone.

Sam has just got angry because Ali has kicked his/her ball over the school fence right at the end of breaktime when most children have already gone into class.

Ali kicks the ball over the fence

↓

Sam gets angry

↓

Sam hits Ali

B) Someone helps Sam to learn the following:
- to recognise the signs that tell him/her s/he is getting angry.
- to take time to calm down.
- if Sam finds it hard to calm down, s/he learns lots of different ways to cool down.
- that it is best to talk to the person that caused the anger after s/he has calmed down.
- that hitting is never a good way to 'sort something out'.
- to think about how his/her violence makes other people feel.
- that talking about things can sort most things out.
- to value a person saying 'sorry'.
- that it is OK to ask for help with tricky situations.

C) Role play
Role-play Sam still getting angry but dealing with this situation in a positive way where nobody gets hurt or upset.

Sam's Story
Questions for discussion

1) Circle any of the following that might be a sign that someone is getting angry.

heart beat gets faster   **breathes more quickly**   **singing**

face goes red   **gritted teeth**   **fists clenched**

forehead wrinkles   **smiles**   **body gets tense**   **shaking**

2) There are two different ways a person can calm down when they are angry. One way is to calm yourself and the other is to use up energy.

What things could Sam do to calm down or use up energy?

Calming:

Using up energy:

3) Why do you think it is not always a good idea for Sam to talk to someone when s/he is angry?

4) Aside from getting angry, what is the actual problem that Sam needs sorting out?

5) What could Sam do to try and get the problem sorted out?

6) We do not know if Ali kicked the ball over the fence deliberately or not.

a) Would this make a difference to how Sam feels?

b) Would this make a difference to what needs to happen to sort out the situation?

Section 2: Putting violent crime into perspective

This section aims to help pupils put violent crime into perspective.

Key questions

- What is violent crime?
- What does the media make us believe about violent crime?
- How does the media report violent crime?
- What is done to prevent violent crime?
- What do we consider works best to prevent violent crime?

Learning objectives of the activities

- to clarify and understand what violent crime is.
- to explore pupils' perception of violent crime.
- to help pupils understand that the media's frequency and methods of reporting crime can give us an unrealistic idea of what is really happening.
- to develop a discerning eye for the way the media portrays violent crime.
- to consider appropriate safety advice for children.
- to be aware of what is being done to prevent crime and consider the effectiveness of some methods.

Learning objectives from the non-statutory guidance for PSHE and Citizenship

Pupils should be taught:

1 a) to talk and write about their opinions, and explain their views, on issues that affect themselves and society

2 b) why and how rules and laws are made and enforced, why different rules are needed in different situations and how to take part in making and changing rules

2 c) to realise the consequences of anti-social and aggressive behaviours, such as bullying and racism, on individuals and communities

2 f) to resolve differences by looking at alternatives, making decisions and explaining choices

2 k) to explore how the media present information

4 a) that their actions affect themselves and others, to care about other people's feelings and to try to see things from their points of view

4 d) to realise the nature and consequences of racism, teasing, bullying and aggressive behaviours, and how to respond to them and ask for help

4 e) to recognise and challenge stereotypes

SPEAKING AND LISTENING

Listening
Pupils should be taught to:
2a. identify the gist of an account or key points in a discussion and evaluate what they hear
2b. ask relevant questions to clarify, extend and follow up ideas
2e. respond to others appropriately, taking into account what they say

Group discussion and interaction
Pupils should be taught to:
3a. make contributions relevant to the topic and take turns in discussion
3c. qualify or justify what they think after listening to others' questions or accounts
3d. deal politely with opposing points of view and enable discussion to move on

READING

Understanding texts
Pupils should be taught to:
2a. use inference and deduction

Reading for information
Pupils should be taught to:
3b. skim for gist and overall impression
3c. obtain specific information through detailed reading
3g. consider an argument critically

Non-fiction and non-literary texts
Pupils should be taught to:
5a. identify the use and effect of specialist vocabulary
5b. identify words associated with reason, persuasion, argument, explanation, instruction and description
5g. engage with challenging and demanding subject matter.

WRITING

Composition
Pupils should be taught to:
1a. choose form and content to suit a particular purpose [for example, notes to read or organise thinking, plans for action, poetry for pleasure]
1b. broaden their vocabulary and use it in inventive ways
1c. use language and style that are appropriate to the reader
1e. use features of layout, presentation and organisation effectively

Planning and drafting
Pupils should be taught to:
2a. plan – note and develop initial ideas
2b. draft – develop ideas from the plan into structured written text

Key Vocabulary
- **violent crime**
- **tabloid**
- **newsworthy**
- **media**

What is violent crime?

Type of activity:
Sorting

Learning objective:
to clarify and understand what violent crime is.

Resources:
Pupil activity sheet 13 'What is violent crime?' (p43); one per pair

1 Give pairs of pupils a copy of the sheet, 'What is violent crime?' (p43) and discuss the definition of violent crime given at the top of the sheet.

2 Explain that everything on the sheet is a crime but that they are not all classified by the law as violent crimes.

3 Ask groups of four to decide which of the crimes on the sheet are violent crimes (B, C, E, F, H, J – because violence is used or threatened) and which are not (A, D, G, I)

4 Ask pupils to feedback their answers and make it clear that if violence is threatened, the police will still classify the crime as a violent one, whether or not violence is actually committed.

5 You could end this activity by asking pupils to write down any questions they have about violent crime and post them into a question box that you have provided. Any issues these questions raise can be used as an informal assessment of pupils' needs and can help guide you when planning future lessons.

Key points:

- Domestic violence is mentioned in E for the purpose of making it very clear that violence in the home against anyone in the family is a crime.
- If pupils mention or ask about rape, you could clarify that it is considered to be a violent crime and that it is defined as one person forcing another person to have sex against their will – most frequently a man forcing a woman to have sex. Many children will have heard this word in news reports, soap operas or other television programmes.

Support/extension:

- Less able pupils could be supported in mixed ability groups.
- Pupils could bring in newspaper clippings of crime reports to compare as violent versus non violent.

Violent crime statistics

Type of activity:
Questionnaire

Learning objective:
to explore pupils' perception of violent crime.

Resources:
Pupil activity sheet 14 'Violent crime statistics– what do you think?' (p44); one per pupil

1 Remind pupils of the definition of violent crime. It might also be necessary to ask pupils if they know what the following words/phrases mean before beginning the task:

injured – hurt
seriously injured – where a person's injury threatens to kill them
vandalism – deliberately damaging public property, e.g., breaking a fence, painting on a wall
burglary – breaking into a building so that you can steal things from it, e.g., breaking into a house to steal the television
theft – stealing something from someone, e.g., pickpocketing

2 Give individual pupils a copy of the sheet 'Violent crime statistics – what do you think?' (p44). Ask them to complete it as honestly as they can. You might need to give brief reminder about how percentages work by displaying a visual aid such as a pie chart.

3 Go through the answers:

1) According to the British Crime Survey (BCS) and Police Records, crime has fallen significantly in the last ten years.

2) According to the BCS, theft (including vehicle-related theft) makes up 45% of all crimes.

3) 51%

4) 2% (Note that 'seriously injured' means an injury that is life threatening)

5) 24%

6) 19%

7) a 20-year-old man

8) a 22-year-old man

If pupils tend to overestimate the prevalence of violent crime, ask them why they believe they did this (probably the influence of crime reporting). However, it does not matter if pupils tend to under, over or accurately estimate the answers. The questions show that violent crime is not extremely prevalent – not as prevalent as our media would lead us to believe.

4 Ask the whole class if any of the statistics shocked them and if so, why.

Key points:

- The vast majority of crimes involve theft and damage of property – not violent crime.
- The majority of victims and offenders of violent crime are young males.
- Crime statistics (from Police Records and the British Crime Survey) only include young people aged 16 and above so they do not indicate crime levels for the under 16s, which some organisations believe are increasing.
- There are areas of Britain, such as large cities, in which violent crime is more prevalent than others.
- There are measures an individual can take to make the chances of being a victim of violent crime very unlikely and there are behaviours and actions that can increase their chance of being a victim of violent crime. These measures include obvious things such as not walking in the streets alone at night, keeping valuable possessions out of sight, using a door chain before you answer the door. A full list of crime prevention methods can be found at http://www.homeoffice.gov.uk/crime-victims/how-you-can-prevent-crime/

Support/extension:

- For pupils that struggle with percentages, it might be a good idea to start by showing a visual representation of what 2%, 10%, 20%, 50%, 75% and 90% would look like approximately. If less able pupils can understand that the smaller the number the smaller the proportion, this should suffice, and the activity can still be used to deliver the learning objective.
- More able pupils could investigate crime statistics on the Internet.

ACTIVITY 3

Type of activity:
Research

Learning objective:
to consider the content of a week's news and how it presents a distilled view of the world.

What does a typical week's news look like?

What to do:

1 Each day, ask pupils to listen to or watch a national news programme and/or collect newspaper clippings (during the school day or as homework). Ask pupils to list the stories that are covered.

2 You could ask pupils to try and put the stories they have listed into different categories. For example: crime, politics, war and terrorism, celebrity, environment, health, finance, natural disasters, good news.

3 At the end of the week, discuss what was covered that week. Ask pupils:
- Did or will any of the stories affect you directly – as an individual? If so, in what

ways? For example, a story about changes in education would eventually have a direct effect on the pupils.

- Overall, how did the stories make you feel about the world you live in?
- Did any of the stories scare you? If so, why?

4 Use the key points to help discuss the pupils' responses to these questions further.

Key points:

- In any one day, news reporters have a choice of stories from around the world because communications are so quick and easy. When pupils consider the stories they have listened to or watched, they will see that they come from a wide variety of places. This means a reporter can pick and choose from a huge 'pot' of stories. What ends up in a newspaper is a condensed version of the world's most notable and extreme happenings. It would be extremely unlikely to see all the events happening in any one person's home community reported in a newspaper.
- One direct effect of news stories is that a person can get a distorted view of the world because so many shocking stories are presented. This can make people scared of the world they live

in – regardless of how safe their community might be.

Support/extension:

- At step 2 of the activity, less able pupils may need the teacher to talk through examples in each category first. They could be given a tally sheet to total up the different types of stories covered in the news or work with a more able partner.
- Pupils could repeat the activity for a local news programme/local newspapers and compare their findings to the national programme.
- Pupils could bring in local papers for a week/month, and then display the stories in the classroom, in categories, to get a visual representation of the news coverage.

ACTIVITY **4**

What makes something newsworthy?

What to do:

1 Give pairs of pupils the sheet 'What makes something newsworthy?' (p45). Read through and discuss each story.

2 Explain to pupils that these stories came from what we call 'tabloid' newspapers as opposed to 'broadsheet' newspapers. A tabloid newspaper could be described as a newspaper that is small in size, giving the news in a condensed (not overly detailed) and often sensational way. Broadsheets tend to be larger, have more serious content and are less likely to use shocking headlines to grab the attention of their readers.

3 Next ask pupils, in small groups, to discuss the questions on the sheet, 'What makes something newsworthy? Questions for discussion (p46). If possible, you could cut out further stories from newspapers and look at what made each one 'newsworthy' before pupils discuss questions 3 and 4.

Type of activity:
Considering news text

Learning objective:
to consider what makes a story newsworthy, why violence is thought to be newsworthy and how it impacts our view of the world.

Resources:
Pupil activity sheet 15 'What makes something newsworthy?' (p45); one per pair, and Pupil activity sheet 16 'What makes something newsworthy? Questions for discussion' (p46); one per group

Answers:

1 a) Story C   **b)** The story is very ordinary and 'everyday', and therefore not particularly interesting.

2) The order in the second column of the table should be: E, A, F, B, D

3) Newsworthy stories can be:
- shocking
- where someone has been treated unfairly
- a story with an interesting twist or angle

- stories that make you feel sorry for someone
- a story about a celebrity
- 'people' stories
- scandalous
- a really tragic story
- stories that scare us – 'scaremongering'
- emotional
- a story involving many people that can be interviewed for their experiences of the event
- stories that imply there will be a direct effect on all of us
- heart wrenching
- a story that no other newspaper managed to get – 'an exclusive'
- dramatic
- where a crime has been committed – especially violent crime.
- a story experts can give more information about
- a story that can last several days or weeks
- a story that tells us about something we had no idea about
- a story that is clear and easy to understand (and not vague)

4) Newspaper stories can influence how we see the world. The person on the alien planet would believe Earth was eventful, dangerous, the behaviour of its people rather extreme, mostly unhappy, etc.

4 Ask pupils to consider why violent crime is likely to make its way into the papers (it ticks many of the boxes for newsworthiness).

5 Develop the discussion about the influence the media has upon us and our view of the world using the ideas highlighted in the key points below.

Key points:

- Newspapers are in competition to sell their papers. They therefore try very hard to get the stories that are going to be of most interest to their readers. The culture of the British tabloid press is such that this usually means they are looking for stories with the most impact to shock and/or cause outrage.
- National newspapers tend to include considerably more bad than good news. Bad news and shocking headlines appear to sell more papers.
- Newspapers have to report their stories quickly. This does not always mean a topic they are reporting will have been researched or even well considered. The press is full of bias (can be political or involve presenting just one viewpoint to make the story as shocking as it can be).
- Violent crimes frequently make the newspapers. A truly shocking violent crime will usually be the top story in a paper for several days (until it loses its shock value or another bigger story comes along).

Support/extension:

- In place of question 3 on the sheet 'What makes something newsworthy? Questions for discussion (p45), less able pupils could be given the following list of words and phrases and decide whether they could be used to describe a newspaper story or not: boring, shocking, ordinary, scandalous, everyday, unusual, dreadful, cheerful.
- Pupils could write a list of story headlines that you would never find in a tabloid newspaper because they are completely non-newsworthy. For example: 'Woman walks her dog' or 'Another sunny day'.
- Read the following story and ask pupils to discuss why they believe the newspaper eventually closed down. Pupils could also make up some headlines that could have been found in such a newspaper.

Good News newspaper

A good news newspaper called Good News was founded because, its American proprietors believed, people were tired of reading bad news. The bi-weekly paper refused to publish any bad news and only printed the good.

It didn't last very long, however. After just 16 months in operation the paper closed down. But it stuck to its guns of publishing only good news to the bitter end and refused to announce its own failure – this would have been contrary to its policy to include no news but good news. The last issue contained the headline "No war declared in 16 weeks".

How does the media report violent crime?

Type of activity:
Discussion and debate prompted by headlines

Learning objective:
to consider how the media uses language and ideas to shock people, and the impact this has on us.

Resources:
Pupil activity sheet 17 'How does the media report violent crime?' (p47); one per pair

What to do:

1 Give pairs of pupils a copy of the sheet 'How does the media report violent crime?' (p47) and discuss the paragraph at the top of the sheet. Reiterate that the key issue for newspapers is to sell as many as possible and try to 'hook' people with their headlines – especially the ones on the front cover.

2 Ask groups of pupils to consider each headline, describe what it is saying in their own words and think about how it is trying to shock the reader. Help pupils conclude that it is sometimes the use of language as well as the ideas that aim to shock us and make things seem very extreme.
- Language examples: menace, tidal wave, soar, true scale, swamp.
- Shocking idea examples: women are getting more violent, gatecrashers are killing people at their wedding (you're not safe anywhere), teenagers are being stabbed, parents are being stabbed.

3 Ask groups of pupils to imagine what idea of the world these headlines would give someone if they were the only thing that person read.

4 Read out the following:

The last government report on violent crime (The British Crime Survey, 2006/7) showed that violent crime had fallen by about 10% in a year. However, some people in the UK believe that it is extremely unsafe to leave their houses.

5 Ask pupils to debate whether they think the media has caused this fear or not.

Key points:
- Some people believe media reports have contributed to people feeling unrealistically afraid of violent crime.
- Although violent crimes clearly do happen and an individual's risk of being a victim of violent crime varies depending on factors like age, sex, address, the impression that stories in the newspapers can leave us with can give us an exaggerated view of our level of personal risk from violent crime. This in turn can make some people feel unsafe when they leave their home – even if the true risk of harm is minimal.

Support/extension:
- Pupils could look at more headlines and unpick how they try to 'hook' people and what impression of the world they can give.
- Pupils could write a letter to a newspaper to complain about 'sensationalism' and request a 'good news page'.

ACTIVITY 6

Type of activity:
Challenging viewpoints

Learning objective:
to consolidate previous learning about putting crime into perspective

Resources:
Pupil activity sheet 18 'Views on violent crime' (p48); one per pair

Views on violent crime

What to do:

1 Give pairs of pupils the sheet 'Views on violent crime' (p48)

2 Ask groups of pupils to develop advice for each person on the sheet. Encourage pupils to use the facts and ideas that they have gathered from the last few activities about violent crime.

For example:
• violent crime is decreasing
• there are things an individual can do to minimise their personal risk
• the media gives us an exaggerated view about the prevalence of violent crime
• if you hear about a violent crime in your area it can be shocking but it doesn't usually mean that the likelihood of an individual being at risk from harm is any greater
• those at greatest risk of becoming a victim of violent crime are men below the age of 24.

3 Ask some pupils to share the advice they would give to each person and discuss this as a whole class.

Key points:

• Sometimes the perception of risk from violent crime is far greater than the reality. Some people would say the media has caused this imbalance.

Support/extension:

• Less able pupils could be given the following prompts to help them develop their advice: How do newspapers report crime? What do these reports make people think is happening in the world? What can you say to these people that would persuade them that they are not in great danger from violent crime?
• Pupils could investigate adults' perceptions of violent crime using the sheet 'Violent crime statistics – what do you think?' (p44) and/or a questionnaire they have designed. They could then display their findings.

ACTIVITY 7

Type of activity:
Problem solving

Learning objective:
to consider appropriate safety advice for children (that would minimise the risk of the very rare incidents of child abduction). This activity is particularly appropriate should a child abduction be receiving considerable press coverage.

Resources:
Pupil activity sheet 19 'Keeping safe' (p49) ; one per pair

Keeping safe

What to do:

1 Give pairs of pupils a copy of the sheet Keeping safe' (p49) and read through the paragraphs at the top of the sheet. Stress all the key points: that there are only a small number of these adults and such incidents are rare. There are things children can do to make themselves more safe.

2 Discuss the situations at the bottom of the page and ask pairs of pupils to make suggestions for each child.

3 Then, as a final consolidation, ask pairs of pupils to write some top tips (for children) for keeping yourself safe when you are out and about.

These should include:
• Keeping parents/carers informed about: who you are with, where you are going, when you will be back and if possible, a phone number that you can be reached at.
• Never going off with an adult unless it has been arranged by your parents/carers beforehand.
• Keeping physically away from any situation that you feel might be dangerous (e.g. a person in a car asking for directions).
• Knowing your full name, address and phone number.

- Arranging a meeting place that you can go to in case you get lost, if you are in a busy place with someone,
- Knowing that you can ask directions or help from a police officer or a shopkeeper.
- Always looking confident and like you know what you are doing if someone approaches you and you are not sure what the person is up to. Bullies and dangerous adults are more likely to pick on a child that does not look confident.

Key points:

- Media coverage of child abductions is extensive and, as with other extreme crimes, this can give people the impression that such crimes are far more common than they really are.
- This activity needs to be finely balanced between reassuring pupils that encountering a dangerous adult is extremely rare and also equipping them with tools to maximise their safety.

- Safety tips can be found at www. juniorcitizen.org.uk 'think safe'

Support/extension:

- Less able pupils could be given a choice of actions for each of the scenarios: e.g. run away, find another adult/an adult that is looking after children, phone home.
- There are many websites devoted to child safety when out and about. Pupils could explore such sites to check that they have included everything in their top tips.

ACTIVITY 8

Tackling violent crime – a case study

Type of activity:
Considering a media report

Learning objective:
to be aware that considerable effort is put into tackling the issue of violent crime, and that prevention activities rarely get the media coverage that crimes receive.

Resources:
Pupil activity sheet 20 'Tackling violent crime – Cumbria Police' (p50); one per pair

What to do:

1 Read through the report, 'Tackling violent crime – Cumbria Police' (p50) as a whole class, up to the 'stars'. There are many words and phrases that might need clarifying for pupils.

2 Ask pupils to consider what this team of police officers might do to prevent drunken violence. Discuss these ideas as a class and list any that the whole class agree are a good idea.

3 Read through the rest of the report together, again checking for understanding as you read.

4 Ask groups of pupils to underline all the actions that Cumbria Police have taken to tackle the issue of violent crime on Friday and Saturday nights. These include:
- More police on the streets on Friday and Saturday nights in places where they can be seen.
- Police in the places where the violent crime usually happens.
- Police will wear headcams to record evidence.
- Police will try and get in early – before a situation gets violent.
- The police will visit pubs and clubs regularly – so they are seen and so they can deal with any situation.
- Police will work with pub owners.
- Police will make a record of trouble spots.
- Police will stop more alcohol being sold to people who are really drunk.
- Police will prevent alcohol being sold to anyone underage.
- Police will make sure anyone who commits a violent crime because of alcohol will be banned from pubs.
- Police have made tackling violent crimes a priority.

5 Ask pupils to discuss their lists and explain how each action will help to prevent violent crime.

6 Ask pupils to consider how the media reports violent crime.
- Does it often report the actions the police take to prevent violent crime?
- How does this add to our picture of violent crime having spiralled out of control?
- Do pupils think these measures should get more media coverage? Why?

Key points:

- A lot of public money is spent trying to reduce crime.
- Cumbria Police have set out to tackle the issue of violence fuelled by alcohol using a variety of methods – including working together with pub owners.
- Crime prevention does not get a lot of media coverage (unless it is controversial). This can lead people to believe that the police do very little and add to the idea that crime is not being tackled or prevented.
- In the UK each year, 45% of violent crime is linked to drunkenness.

Support/extension:

- The text in the report is difficult in places and the whole class could work together to summarise the key points. These could be recorded.
- If possible, a local police officer (or PCSO) could visit to talk about violence that is induced by drunkenness. This could be part of drug and alcohol education. They could also talk about crime prevention measures in the local area, with a focus of violence.

ACTIVITY 9

Type of activity:
Discussion

Learning objective:
to consider what might work to combat violent crime, and to appreciate that this can be an area of controversy.

Resources:
Pupil activity sheet 21 'Tackling violent crime – what works?' (p51); one per pair

Tackling violent crime – what works?

What to do:

1 Explain to pupils that a lot of money and time is devoted to crime prevention. Despite this, violent crimes do still happen, so there is still a need to find what works best in stopping them.

2 Give pairs of pupils a copy of the sheet 'Tackling violent crime – what works?' (p51). Explain that all the suggestions are just opinions that some people would not agree with. Be sure that pupils understand the significance of these statements being opinions and not factual information. Ask groups of mixed ability pupils to consider each opinion and discuss why another person might disagree with each suggestion. For example, objections might be:
- Keeping people in prison costs a lot of money.
- It can be dangerous if a person in a community tries to stop a violent crime.
- Why should public money be used to entertain young people?
- Some parents just don't have the skills to control their children.
- A victim would be scared to meet their attacker – and scared they might attack again.
- Labelling offenders can prevent them from turning over a new leaf.
- Knowing where crimes are committed does not stop them from happening.
- If you let people report anonymously, they might just make things up.
- Police need to make records so they have information to help them solve crimes.
- CCTV means we are being watched all the time – we are not all criminals.
- Schools have enough to do, they cannot be responsible for everything a child does or how they turn out.

3 As a whole class discuss these opinions and ensure the controversies are explored.

- The controversy in crime prevention is around whose responsibility it is to prevent crime, which methods actually work, how much different methods cost, and how far we can go to limit a convicted criminal's personal freedom.
- All individuals are different – so what works to prevent crime for one might not work for another.
- Keeping the public safe always needs to be a consideration in crime prevention.

- Pupils could investigate articles on the internet to find out why the following are controversial: CCTV, tagging criminals, parents/carers being fined for their children's behaviour, the effectiveness of ASBOs (anti-social behaviour orders) and ABCs (acceptable behaviour contracts).

What is violent crime?

A **violent crime** is a crime in which the *offender* deliberately uses or *threatens* to use violent force upon the *victim*. Violent crimes include crimes *committed* with and without weapons.

Which of the following do you think are violent crimes?

A A person taking someone's wallet from their pocket as they walk past them in the street.	**B** A man entering a post office with a metal rod and threatening to smash the glass counter unless the person behind it hands over all the money.
C Someone punching another person with the intention of starting a fight.	**D** Someone painting graffiti on a road sign.
E A man hitting his wife because she burnt his dinner.	**F** A bank robbery where guns are fired but nobody is injured.
G Someone stealing an empty car by forcing the window open.	**H** Someone stabbing another person with a knife.
I A person being injured in an accidental car crash because the driver wasn't paying enough attention.	**J** Someone pushing a person up against a wall and threatening to hurt them if they do not hand over their money.

Word meanings:

offender: the person that commits the crime.
victim: the person who has the crime done to them.
threaten: make a person feel at risk of danger by what you are doing or saying.
committed: done.

Violent crime statistics – what do you think?

Read each question and circle the answer you believe is correct.

1 Do you think there is more or less violent crime than ten years ago?

more   less

2 Which of the following crimes do you think happens the most?

vandalism   violent crime   burglary   theft

3 What percentage of violent crimes do you think end up with someone being injured?

3%   51%   75%   92%

4 What percentage of violent crimes do you think end up with a person being *seriously hurt* (in other words, the injury threatens to kill them)?

2%   10%   67%   98%

5 What percentage of violent crimes do you think involve some kind of weapon?

24%   52%   73%   98%

6 Approximately what percentage of violent crimes do you think involve the use of a knife or sharp object?

19%   45%   55%   84%   99%

7 Which of the following do you think is most likely to be a victim of violent crime?

a 19-year-old woman   a 20-year-old man   a 78-year-old woman
a 40-year-old man   a 10-year-old boy

8 Which of the following do you think is most likely to be arrested for committing a violent crime?

a 13-year-old boy   a 22-year-old man
a 30-year-old man   a 40-year-old woman

SHEET 15

What makes something newsworthy?

A

Honeymoon horror: Groom plunges to his death from hotel balcony

A heartbroken bride today prepared to fly home with the body of her husband, who died after falling from a hotel balcony on their honeymoon.

Dave Arnold, 32, died on Tuesday night after falling six floors from the balcony in Spain.

He was on honeymoon with his wife Kate Arnold, 29, whom he married a week ago in Taunton, Somerset.

B

Female celebs get claws out

This exclusive snap shows fiery celebrity Philippa Penze landing herself in a nasty catfight with a fellow clubber last Sunday.

The scary incident happened at a London nightspot, when a mystery brunette apparently attacked the reality star.

C

OLD MAN GETS THE WRONG CHANGE

Ron Peters, 76, was handed the wrong change when he popped to his local shop to buy a loaf of bread.

"The bread cost 97 pence, I handed over a pound and the lady behind the counter gave me just a penny in change. This is clearly wrong."

People were happy to discover that the further two pence Ron was owed was returned to him later that day.

D

HEROIC DAD DIES TRYING TO RESCUE A SCHOOLGIRL

A courageous father-of-two drowned while trying to save the life of a schoolgirl. Sanjeev Gupta, 42, of Reigate, Surrey, saw the 14-year-old struggling to stay afloat.

Safety equipment had been vandalised and removed. So, ignoring warning signs, he jumped in but was pulled under by a strong current.

E

OAP woman celebrates £3.8m lottery win – by buying new knees

For the lottery multi-millionaire, it must be a difficult choice. Which little luxury should we go for first – the mansion, the limo or the world cruise?

After recovering from the shock of taking a £3,808, 401 share in a rollover jackpot, Margaret Binns got straight on the phone to the nearest private hospital to book herself in for replacement knees.

Margaret, 69 has been on the NHS waiting list for an operation and suffers constant pain.

F

The killer of a headteacher swaggers down the street free as a bird after just 10 years in jail

Evil Chad Mazzei, 24, was photographed in North London on temporary release from prison.

Mazzei was jailed for life in January 1998 for stabbing the dad-of-two to death.

He looked relaxed and unfazed by his new-found freedom as he strolled among shoppers seemingly oblivious to his presence.

SECTION 2: PUTTING VIOLENT CRIME INTO PERSPECTIVE

45

What makes something newsworthy?

Questions for discussion

Newsworthy: worth reporting in the news because it could be of interest.

1 a) Which one of these stories does not seem like something you would find in a newspaper?
b) Why do you think this?

2 Match each of the stories with what made it newsworthy.

The newsworthy bit..	Letter
Someone won lots of money but it was shocking to find that they used that money to pay for something that should be free.	
Someone died tragically at a time that they would usually be really happy.	
Someone committed a terrible crime but it seems as though they have not been punished properly for it.	
Someone famous was behaving in a shocking way.	
Someone died being really brave and trying to save a young person.	

3 List some adjectives or phrases that could be used to describe the type of stories newspapers like to report.
Here are three to start you off.
• shocking
• where someone has been treated unfairly
• a story with an interesting twist

Notes

4 Imagine someone lived on an alien planet and only read tabloid newspapers to get their information about the planet Earth. What would the papers lead them to believe Earth was like?

SHEET 17 How does the media report violent crime?

The people that produce newspapers want to sell as many as they can. Headlines on the front of newspapers try to grab people's attention so that they buy the newspaper. However, these shocking headlines can be scary and give us an exaggerated view of what is happening outside our front doors.

Consider each of the following headlines one at a time and:

1 describe what the headline is saying in your own words

2 think about how the headline is trying to shock us.

KNIFE MENACE EVERY 4 MINUTES

RIVERS OF BLOOD

UK GUN CRIME EVERY HOUR

Tidal wave of violent crime

Violent crime figures soar

By the time you've read this page another person will be a knife victim

Cops say knife crime is worsening

Mother of stabbed teenager tells of her shock

Exclusive: Police memo reveals true scale of knife crime

Bridegroom stabbed at own wedding by gatecrasher

RISING VIOLENT CRIME TIDE

Police beaten by litter rage mob

STAB VICTIMS SWAMP THE NHS

Crimes go unpunished by our courts

KNIFE AND GUN CRIME WORSENING

Violence in women at record high

GANG KILLED DAD IN FEUD OVER ASSAULT

Views on violent crime

What could you say to these people to make them feel better or challenge their viewpoints?

"There was a stabbing in our city last week. I thought it was a safe place to be because we have never had anything like this before. I will now think twice before I go into the city."

Janice, aged 32

"Not a day goes by when there isn't a story about some violent crime splashed across the front of the newspaper. Violent crime is just getting worse and worse. I feel really unsafe to leave my home."

Mehmet, aged 66

"It seems like every young person goes out with a knife or a gun these days."

Jamie, aged 20

Keeping safe

There are a small number of adults in the world that would deliberately harm children. The crimes these adults commit are very, very rare. However, when they do commit a crime the newspapers report it at length. For this reason you might have heard of a crime where a child has been 'stolen' by one of these adults.

These adults are mentally ill and tragically do not have the same idea of right and wrong as most people. This is why they can do such terrible things. These adults are sometimes called 'dangerous adults'.

While it is important to remember that these crimes are extremely rare, it is also important for children to know how to keep themselves safe and make the chances of ANYTHING bad happening to them very, very unlikely.

What would you suggest the following children do?

Gary is playing football in the street. A woman that he has seen before but that he doesn't know suggests that he goes with her. She says that Gary's mum has asked her to fetch him. What should Gary do? 	Mehmet is 6. She went to the park with her older brother but he went off with his friends and she cannot find him anywhere. She doesn't know her way home. What should he do? 
Katie is 7 and is at her friend Catarina's house. Catarina's mum usually walks Katie home but she hasn't got back from work yet. It is dark outside and she is due home by 5 p.m. It is already 4:50 p.m. and the walk home takes at least 20 minutes. What should Katie do? 	Lubna is walking home from school. Just ahead of her, next to the curb, there is a car parked with its passenger door open. A man is sitting inside. What should she do? 

Tackling violent crime – Cumbria Police

Cumbria Constabulary is to run an operation aimed at reducing violent crime in Kendal. Operation Sapphire will run throughout September and aims to reduce the number of assaults with injury in the town.

The operation is timed to coincide with a traditional rise in the number of assaults with injury that occur at this time of year and will focus on hotspot areas such as Highgate, Strammondgate and Branthwaite Brow.

High visibility teams of officers will police the town centre on Friday and Saturday nights when alcohol-fuelled violence tends to erupt.

****

Officers will be deployed with headcams to gather footage that can be used as evidence, but will focus on early intervention, with officers tackling incidents early before they lead to violent situations. Officers will attempt to prevent people's behaviour escalating into something more serious.

Structured pub and club visits will be introduced to maintain a visible presence inside licensed premises, as well as on the streets, and a register will be maintained to help officers identify trouble spots and work with licensees to reduce violent and drunken behaviour.

The operation will also target the root cause of many of these incidents by enforcing the non-sale of alcohol to people who are clearly drunk, and by tackling proxy sales, where adults purchase alcohol on behalf of people under 18, who can then drink on the streets and start causing trouble.

"There is nothing wrong with drinking alcohol, but there is everything wrong with using it as an excuse to let high spirits turn into aggressive behaviour." said Inspector Neil Allison, who is coordinating the operation.

"We will be enforcing the law robustly, and will refer all incidents where alcohol was an aggravating factor to our local Pubwatch scheme to ensure that offenders are banned from local licensed premises."

Chief Superintendent Paul Kennedy added: "Cumbria Constabulary is committed to building safer and stronger communities in South Cumbria, so tackling violent crime is a top priority for officers in the area.

"We should not allow a minority of people to ruin the enjoyment of the majority of people who want to enjoy the nightlife that Kendal and other towns have to offer without the fear of violent crime."

The number of violent crimes reported to police in South Cumbria is falling, but officers want to reduce that figure even further.

Assaults with injury do not always lead to serious injury, but any kind of aggressive behaviour is unacceptable and officers will be enforcing all related incidents robustly.

SHEET 21 — Tackling violent crime – what works?

People hold quite different views about what stops violent crime from happening.

Here are some suggestions different people have made:

You need to keep people in prison for longer. Punishments are what stop people from committing crimes.

Communities need to look out for each other more and protect each other.

There need to be more things for young people to get involved in, like youth clubs. If you got them putting their energy into positive things, they would be less likely to commit crimes.

I think parents need to be made more responsible for their children's actions; parents should be fined if they don't control their children properly.

If someone commits a violent crime, they should be made to meet their victim. That will help them understand the harm they have done.

Criminals should have their names, photographs and details about their crimes printed in the papers so everyone knows who they are and what they did.

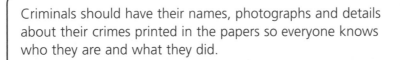

People should be given maps and leaflets that show them where lots of crimes happen so they can avoid these places.

People are scared of reporting violent crimes in case they get attacked again. People should be allowed to report things anonymously.

You should make anyone that has committed a violent crime wear something so everyone knows who they are.

You just need more police out and about everywhere. If they had less paperwork to do – they'd be able to police more.

There needs to be more CCTV recording what happens on our streets.

Schools need to be teaching their pupils right from wrong.

SECTION 3

Violence in the media

The aim of this section is to give children a discerning eye for the violence included in screen media.

Key questions

- Why is there so much violence in films, on the TV and in computer games?
- What are our attitudes to screen violence?
- How does watching violence affect us and others?
- Should TV companies or parents control what their children watch?

Learning objectives of the activities

- to explore pupils' perceptions of screen violence.
- to understand why action films are so prevalent in the film industry.
- to consider why so much violence is portrayed in screen media.
- to consider how watching violence might affect us.
- to develop a discerning eye for the violence portrayed in screen media.
- to consider the age classifications of films and whether they prevent young children from viewing violent material.

Learning objectives from the non-statutory guidance for PSHE and Citizenship

Pupils should be taught:
1 a) to talk and write about their opinions, and explain their views, on issues that affect themselves and society
2 b) why and how rules and laws are made and enforced, why different rules are needed in different situations and how to take part in making and changing rules
2 k) to explore how the media present information

SPEAKING AND LISTENING

Listening
Pupils should be taught to:

2a identify the gist of an account or key points in a discussion and evaluate what they hear

2b ask relevant questions to clarify, extend and follow up ideas

2e respond to others appropriately, taking into account what they say

Group discussion and interaction
Pupils should be taught to:

3a. make contributions relevant to the topic and take turns in discussion

3b. vary contributions to suit the activity and purpose, including exploratory and tentative comments where ideas are being collected together, and reasoned, evaluative comments as discussion moves to conclusions or actions

3c. qualify or justify what they think after listening to others' questions or accounts

3d. deal politely with opposing points of view and enable discussion to move on

READING

Understanding texts
Pupils should be taught to:

2a. use inference and deduction

Reading for information
Pupils should be taught to:

3b. skim for gist and overall impression

3c. obtain specific information through detailed reading

3g. consider an argument critically

Non-fiction and non-literary texts
Pupils should be taught to:

5g. engage with challenging and demanding subject matter.

Key vocabulary
- screen media
- screen violence
- genres

Screen violence

Type of activity:
Drawing and labelling

Learning objective:
to explore pupils' perception of screen violence

What to do:

1 Ask pupils to think about any violence they have seen on **television**, in **films**, in **cartoons**, in **computer games**, or on **the Internet.** Ask them to draw a picture of the violence. If they claim to have never seen violence, ask them to draw what they believe violence in films or games might be like.

2 Ask pupils to label their pictures using the following prompts:
• What type of violence have you drawn? (e.g., gun/weapon use, punching)
• Have you drawn an injury? If so what type of injury is it? (e.g., blood, bruise)
• Where have you seen violence like this – has it come from a particular programme, game, etc?

3 Ask pupils to work in groups of four and explore what they have drawn. They should take it in turns to explain what they have drawn and then, as a group, put their pictures in order from the picture they believe is the most to the least violent.

4 Ask each group to explain the reasons behind their ordering. These might include:
• How lethal the weapons are considered to be – if weapons are used.
• How gory the injuries are.
• How the injured party is left (dead, injured, distressed or exactly as they were before the violence).
• How realistic the violence is (e.g., if it's in a cartoon it might not be deemed as violent as if it were in a film). This could be debated by imagining the cartoon violence acted out by actors.
• Whether what is portrayed is real and actually happened (e.g., a boxing fight) or fantasy.
• How much force is portrayed.
• How long the violence lasts.
• How often the violence happens.
• How defenceless the victim is.

5 As a whole class open up discussion in response to the question:
• What makes something in screen media seem really violent?

Key points:

• Most children and young people have been exposed to some screen media violence. The pictures pupils draw will give you an indication of the media violence pupils have been exposed to and can inform your future planning.
• There is a lot of violence portrayed in screen media. Different portrayals can seem more violent than others depending on a number of factors, some of which are outlined above.

Support/extension:

• Less confident artists could use stick people in their pictures.
• Pupils could draw or make a violence spectrum, showing what the class deemed the least violent portrayals of violence to the most violent. They could label the features that determine the position of each portrayal on the spectrum.

Type of activity:
Sorting activity
followed by discussion

Learning objective:
to realise that there is
controversy about the
effect screen violence
has on people.

Resources:
Pupil activity sheet 22
'How might watching
screen violence affect
us?' (p58); one per pair

How might watching screen violence affect us?

What to do:

1 Give pairs of pupils a copy of the sheet 'How might watching screen violence affect us?' (p58). Introduce Ash and Pat. Ash believes that screen violence is exciting and does not have any bad effects on the people who watch it. Pat thinks screen violence is unnecessary and that it does have a bad effect on the people who watch it. Explain that we don't know whether Ash and Pat are male or female. You could ask pupils to speculate and challenge any stereotyping.

2 Ask small groups of pupils to sort the quotes on the page into those Ash probably said and those Pat probably said:
• PAT: b,c,d,e,i
• ASH: a,f,g,h,j

3 Go through the answers with the whole class. Summarise the points both Ash and Pat have made in a table with the headings 'For screen violence' and 'Against screen violence'.

4 Ask individual pupils to consider where they stand in this debate, i.e. do they agree more with Ash or Pat?

5 Open up a whole-class discussion and end with pupils voting on whether they believe screen violence does or does not affect people. Don't forget to offer the option of abstaining as this is an issue the experts still cannot agree on!

Key points:

• Sometimes there are claims in the media that an individual's violent behaviour has been directly caused by screen violence. However, many people watch screen violence and never commit violent acts.
• This issue is controversial. Many people say there is not a straightforward link between screen violence and people's behaviour and that there are many other factors determining whether or not an individual will commit a violent act as a result of screen violence, e.g., mental health, input from the people in someone's life.

Support/extension:

• Less able pupils could either be included in mixed ability groups, work with support or be given fewer quotes to sort.
• Pupils could make up extra quotes that Ash and Pat might have said.

Type of activity:
Investigation guided by
questions

Learning objective:
to develop a critical eye
for screen violence.

A close look at screen violence

What to do:

1 Give individual pupils the sheet 'A close look at screen violence' (p59). Read through the questions and check pupils' understanding.

2 Ask pupils to think of an example of screen violence they have seen, perhaps the one they drew in the earlier activity, 'Screen violence' (p59). This activity could also be set as a week's homework and pupils could complete the sheet as and when they encounter screen violence at home.

3 Ask pupils to try and answer all of the questions for their example of screen violence. For a few examples of screen violence, some of the questions might be hard to answer, but encourage pupils to consider all of the questions.

4 When pupils have answered the questions, ask small groups of pupils to use their answers to consider the question:
• In what way is screen violence not like real violence?

5 Discuss their answers as a whole class and consider how screen violence can give us a slightly warped impression of violence. Use the key points below to guide the discussion.

Key points:

• Screen violence is not like real violence in the following ways:

1 Screen violence is usually more prevalent (and relentless) than real violence.

2 Screen violence can be more graphic than anything we would be likely to see when we walk down the street.

3 Screen violence often has unreal consequences. For example: a person is injured but the 'story' just carries on, no one gets arrested, people receive an injury but recover immediately.

4 Screen violence varies in how realistic it is, e.g. cartoons can be very unrealistic.

5 Screen violence is often portrayed as justified, committed by a goodie against a baddie and often the only solution to a situation.

6 Screen violence can be glamorised, i.e. the violence seems cool and exciting.

• Computer games use violence in a variety of ways and this could be explored (with sensitivity to those pupils who do not access computer games at home):

1 The different genres of game mean that a person can be committing violence (e.g., shooting) in the first person or controlling a fight as if they are watching from the side.

2 Some sports games get a lower age rating because they are sport. However, some of these (e.g., boxing games) can show incredibly graphic injuries.

3 Some games allow the player to make up their own characters.

This can include making a character that looks very like themselves. This character then becomes a victim and/ or perpetrator of violence.

4 With games linking up to an online network, players can now interact with other players and can end up as a member of one side fighting another. With single player settings (offline), the player is often a 'goodie' fighting 'baddies'.

5 Some computer games use high technology science to make how a person moves as a result of an injury extremely realistic.

6 Many computer games use a variety of extreme weapons and means of causing harm, e.g. guns, fireballs, vehicles running people over.

7 Winning through violence can be glorified.

8 The sound effects as well as the visuals can add to how realistic a game is.

9 You play a computer game to win, not necessarily to have fun.

10 Computer games can be highly addictive.

Support/extension:

• Less able pupils could draw their example of screen violence and label the picture with answers to some of the questions on the sheet.

• Pupils could compare violence in different genres, such as cartoons, the different computer game genres (e.g., FPS, beatemups), TV programmes, action films.

What about age ratings?

Type of activity:
Discussion

Learning objective:
to consider age ratings and whether they work.

Resources:
Pupil activity sheet 24 'What about age ratings?' (p60); one per pair

What to do:

1 Explain to pupils that the British Board of Film Classification (BBFC) views every film and awards it a classification depending upon the age range it believes the film would be suitable for. The classification takes several things into account, including any violent content.

2 Give pairs of pupils a copy of the sheet, 'What about age ratings?' (p60). Talk through the different classifications and what level of violence you would find in each. A full version of the age classifications can be found on the CD-ROM.

3 Next ask pairs of pupils to try and classify the films on the sheet; a brief synopsis of each has been included. The films rated U, PG and 12 are the hardest to categorise without actually seeing the film, but encourage pupils to speculate about which they believe might contain more violence. There is only one film per classification.

4 Once everyone has guessed, give pupils the answers:
• High School Musical – U
• City of Ember – PG
• Eagle Eye – 12A
• Max Payne – 15
• Mum and Dad – 18

5 Next ask pupils to discuss the following questions in pairs or small groups:
  1 Do your parents/carers pay attention to film classifications?
  2 Do you think young children should be prevented from watching violence and if so, why?
  3 Do you think the classifications work to prevent children from watching violence?
  4 Do you think some children think watching films rated 15 or 18 is exciting because it's 'forbidden'?
  5 Do you think extreme violence (e.g. kicking, punching, stabbing or shooting) should be banned from films, the Internet or television?
  6 If you were a parent/carer who disagreed with children watching violence, what would you do to prevent your child from watching it?

6 Take any feedback pupils are willing to volunteer after their discussions.

Key points:

• Some people argue that children can be very disturbed by watching graphic screen violence and that they should be prevented from doing so.
• The film classifications do not always appear to prevent children from accessing films that have been rated 15 and 18.
• Some children believe that watching films with a 15 or 18 rating holds some kudos. This therefore makes older rated films more attractive to some people.
• In the past extremely violent films were censored (i.e.banned to prevent anyone from seeing them). Some people would agree with this kind of censorship, others say that it should be down to individuals to decide what they watch.
• As time goes on, people get used to more and more violence portrayed in films. This means film makers include more and more violence – so that films are still found shocking. For example, a film that was considered extremely violent in the 1950s would seem extremely tame now. Film classifications would reflect this change in attitudes. Furthermore, some films that were banned in the past are considered to be classics now.

Support/extension:

• Pupils could investigate film censorship in the past. What caused something to be censored?
• Further information about film classification can be found at www.bbfc.co.uk

SHEET 22 How might watching screen violence affect us?

Ash

Ash believes that screen violence is exciting and does not have any bad effects on the people who watch it.

Pat

Pat thinks screen violence is unnecessary and thinks it does have a bad effect on the people who watch it.

Sort the following into what you think Ash probably said or what Pat probably said.

a
I think that watching violence does not actually make a person violent. Perhaps it's just that people that are violent already are more likely to want to watch violence.

b
Some computer games show an incredible amount of violence. These can make a person feel really excited, their heart pumps more quickly and they breathe quicker. This can't be good for the body.

c
Some computer programmes let you make up your own characters and what they look like. This means you can put a character that looks like yourself into the programme. This means a character that looks very like yourself commits violence or has violence done to them.

d
You hear kids using phrases, words and actions from violent games when they play. This shows that using these games do affect a person.

e
Computer graphics are so good now, injuries can look so realistic. This can be very disturbing.

f
I think that acting out violence in a computer game takes away the need to be violent in real life.

g
I think kids get a real sense of power and achievement when they play computer games – especially if they are not doing well at school.

h
Most people understand that violence is wrong. Watching screen violence won't make a person suddenly change their mind about that.

i
After watching lots of violence, you become numb to it. Then you can see violence and it has no effect on you and you stop seeing injuries as real.

j
Everyone knows the difference between reality and make-believe.

SHEET 23 — A close look at screen violence

Consider a violent act you have seen in a film, a computer game, on the internet, on the news, in a cartoon, in a soap opera, or any other you can think of. For this act of violence, try to answer each of the following questions.

1 What type of violence was shown? (e.g. hitting, using a weapon, a bomb explosion)

_____
_____
_____
_____
_____
_____

2 How realistic or believable was the violence?

_____
_____
_____
_____
_____
_____

3 Was an injury shown? If so, what was the injury and how gory was it?

_____
_____
_____
_____
_____

4 Was the fact someone was hurt noticed or was no big deal made about it?

_____
_____
_____
_____
_____

5 Was the violence an important part of a story or was it included just for thrills?

_____
_____
_____
_____
_____
_____

6 If you saw the violence happen to people outside your house, would it be acceptable?

_____
_____
_____
_____
_____

7 Was the violence made out to be justified – in other words, the right thing to do?

_____
_____
_____
_____
_____

8 Was the violence committed by a goodie, a baddie or neither?

_____
_____
_____
_____
_____

9 Was the violence made out to be a clever or cool thing to do?

_____
_____
_____
_____
_____

10 Was the violence punished?

_____
_____
_____
_____
_____

What about age ratings?

Most countries have a system that decides the age range that a film or computer game would be suitable for. This is the British system for films:

Mild violence only. Occasional mild threat or menace only.

Moderate violence, without detail, may be allowed, if justified by its setting (e.g., historic, comedy or fantasy).

Violence must not dwell on detail. There should be no emphasis on injuries or blood. Sexual violence may only be implied or briefly and discreetly indicated.

Violence may be strong but may not dwell on the infliction of pain or injury. Scenes of sexual violence must be discreet and brief.

Violence appears to risk harm to individuals or, through their behaviour, to society – e.g., any detailed portrayal of violent or dangerous acts.

What rating do you think the following films were given?

Max Payne

Max Payne is a maverick cop – a mythical anti-hero – determined to track down those responsible for the brutal murders of his family and partner. Hell-bent on revenge, his obsessive investigation takes him on a nightmare journey into a dark underworld. As the mystery deepens, Max is forced to battle enemies beyond the natural world and face an unthinkable betrayal.

High School Musical

America's favourite high school students hit senior year. Amidst a basketball championship, prom and a big spring musical featuring all of the Wildcats, Troy and Gabriella vow to make every moment last as their lifelong college dreams put the future of their relationship in question. A crew of sophomore Wildcats joins in on the fun, new music and dance numbers.

City of Ember

For generations, the people of the City of Ember have flourished in an amazing world of glittering lights. But Ember's once powerful generator is failing..and the great lamps that illuminate the city are starting to flicker. Now, two teenagers, in a race against time, must search Ember for clues that will unlock the ancient mystery of the city's existence, and help the citizens escape before the lights go out forever.

Mum and Dad

Set around London's Heathrow Airport, the film centres on a murderous and perverse family who live in a house at the end of the runway right under the roar of the flight path. They live off the contents of supposedly 'lost' luggage, but the 'family business' is much more sinister...

Eagle Eye

Jerry Shaw and Rachel Holloman are two strangers thrown together by a mysterious phone call from a woman they have never met. Threatening their lives and families, she pushes Jerry and Rachel into a series of increasingly dangerous situations – using the technology of everyday life to track and control their every move. As the situation escalates, these two ordinary people become the country's most wanted fugitives, who must work together to discover what is really happening – and more importantly, why.

Assembly Ideas

These pages outline assemblies that could be delivered using the activities in this book.

Learning objective

- To know that violence is wrong and consider how it can be prevented.

Key Points

- With some exceptions (self defence, soldiers fighting a war and police prevention of violence) violence is always deemed wrong because it harms another person.
- Schools usually have school rules that either directly say or imply that violence is wrong and should not happen.
- There are usually many non-violent choices open to a person to sort out a situation.
- A school might like to declare that it is a zero tolerance zone with respect to violence

Activities

1 Read out to the pupils what school rules, the law and the United Nations says about violence (on p12)

2 Ask the assembly to consider why violence is wrong.

3 Use the Sam's scenario on p30 which highlights how anger can cause a person to become violent. If you have time to pre-prepare, you can ask pupils to act out the scenario to bring it to life.

4 Look at the different ways Sam was taught how not to be violent – as outlined on the sheet. Take each thing Sam learnt one at a time and ask pupils how they think they help Sam not to be violent.

5 Explain to pupils that pupils should be able to come to school without being at risk from violence, that any violence should be reported to an adult and it will be dealt with.

6 Introduce the idea of the school being a zero-tolerance zone and ask pupils what they think this means.

Reflection

Ask pupils to imagine a world with no violence.

Assembly 2

Learning objective

- To consider the situation of 'self defence' in school.

Key Points

- If self defence is defined in a school in the same way as it is in law, it is unlikely that any violent act is truly 'self defence.'
- Hitting in retaliation can often make a situation escalate.
- Most situations have non-violent solutions.
- Sometimes parents/carers say 'just hit them back.' This is rarely the best way to sort a situation out – especially if the adults in a school take anti-violence very seriously and consistently deal with violent incidents.

Activities

1 Ask six responsible pupils to join you at the front of the assembly.

2 Explain that the pupils represent a cartoon strip of some violence that happened at school between just two pupils: pupil A and pupil B.

3 Position the pupils in three pairs and explain to each pair in front of everyone the freeze-frame that they are to produce. There are opportunities for humour at this point.

FRAME 1: Pupil A calls pupil B a nasty name.
FRAME 2: Pupil A hit pupil B.
FRAME 3: Pupil B hit pupil A back

4 Explain how the law defines self defence:
  1 The violence is directed only against someone who is attacking.
  2 The aim of the violence is only to stop the attack.
  3 The violence done in self defence is the only way the attack can be stopped.

5 Ask the assembly to consider whether there was any self defence in this scenario (if you use the legal definition). No!

6 Ask the assembly
- What was the first thing a person did that was 'wrong?' (call pupils B a nasty name)
- What else happened that was 'wrong?' (hitting)
- At which points in the freeze-frame could pupils A and pupils B have decided to do something differently? (after the name calling and after the first hit)
- What else could either pupils A or pupil B have done to make the outcome more positive?

7 Ask two further pupils to come and add a fourth freeze-frame to the hitting scenario. If they fail to have an idea – suggest a full blown fight to show how retaliation can cause things to escalate.

8 Ask the pupils in the second freeze-frame to show a better response to the name calling and the pupils in the third freeze-frame to show a better response to the first hit.

9 Sum up by explaining that violence rarely sorts out anything and there are always better solutions.

Reflection

Ask pupils to imagine a non-violent response to someone calling them a name.

Assembly 3

Learning objective

- To appreciate that the media can give us an inaccurate sense of the prevalence of violent crime.

Key Points

- Newspapers just want lots of people to buy them.
- Newspapers use shocking headlines to try and grab people's attention and get people to buy them.
- Violent crime is nearly always shocking and is often made into a news story.
- The media have pickings from around the world of newsworthy stories. This means they will choose the most extreme stories from a huge selection.
- The media can give us an exaggerated view of the violent crime.

Activities

1 Tell pupils that you have been reading a lot of newspapers recently. Ask them to guess which of the following were headlines that you read in a newspaper and which were not:
- Man stabbed in late night brawl
- Woman completes cardigan with super fast knitting
- Celebrity gets into vicious fight
- Molly Smith gets rabbit keepers girl guide badge
- House fire blaze – kills three
- Kettle broken at number 45 Canley Street
- Post Office robbed at gunpoint
- Tracey takes a new route to school
- Plane crash carnage
- Daisies picked from lawn
- Car crashes into police station
- Mrs Patel eats dinner at 8 instead of 7

2 Ask pupils how they knew which headlines were likely to be in the paper and which were not.

3 Refer to the teachers notes on p36. 'What makes something newsworthy' to explain to pupils that

newspaper companies just want to sell as many newspapers as possible. Tabloids in particular write headlines that try to grab people's attention. They do this usually by trying to shock. Newspapers do not worry about the impact these headlines might have on someone.

4 Ask pupils to imagine if they lived on a desert island and had a tabloid newspaper from Britain delivered to it each day. What impression of Britain do they think they would get.

5 Then ask pupils to visualise a walk down their local street. What are they likely to see? Compare this with the desert island view.

6 Complete the assembly by highlighting that although bad things do happen, the media can lead us to believe that they happen far more often than they do in reality. This can lead some people too scared to leave their house.

Reflection

Ask pupils to think about the idea that we do not always have to believe what we are told.

Assembly 4

Learning objective

- To put any heavily reported violent incident into perspective and teach pupils how to keep safe.

Key Points

- This assembly is appropriate after a high profile child abduction or violent incident against a child has occurred.
- Pupils need to be reassured that these events are rare but they can also be helped to feel better by covering what they can do to help themselves as safe as possible when they are out and about.

Activities

1 Mention the incident that has been reported and express your concern for how tragic the event is.

2 Use the teachers' notes p39 and the boxed writing on the pupils' page 'Keeping Safe' on p49 to help you explain to pupils that dangerous adults do exist but that they are rare. Explain that the media goes 'wild' over stories like these because they are so shocking but that their coverage can leave us with a feeling that the event is on our very doorstep and that it happens a lot.

3 Having said that these events are rare, you can then go on to revise what children can do to decrease the likelihood of them getting into danger using the points covers in the teachers' notes on p39.

Reflection

Ask children to reflect upon all the people in their lives who keep them safe and care about them.

Assembly 5

Learning objective

- To consider how violence is portrayed in screen media This assembly is best carried out with some prior preparation.

Key Points

- Violence is used in films because it sells worldwide (because it's easier to understand than a complex drama or comedy.
- There are huge debates about the effect screen violence has upon a person but it is agreed that the issue is complex and very few individuals that watch screen violence will go on to commit violent acts.
- It is a good idea to equip young people with a discerning eye for the messages they receive from the media.

Activities

1 Ask some pupils (that are comfortable with acting) to prepare some examples of typical screen violence. These might include:
- A cartoon style chase
- A shooting computer game
- A boxing game
- A soap opera
- An American cop movie
- A science fiction fight (e.g. laser guns)

Encourage sound effects!

2 Ask one pair of pupils to be prepared to act out a realistic playground fight.

3 Be sure to insist that there is no actual hitting.

4 Using the questions found on p59 'A close look at screen violence, point out how the violent in films, games and on TV are not, thankfully, realistic and it happens with more force and frequency than in real life. Compare the playground fight to the violence found in screen media to highlight different levels of reality.

5 Ask pupils to consider how this violence makes people feel.

6 As pupils to imagine living in a violent film or computer game. Would the action seem acceptable?

7 Complete the assembly by explaining to pupils that the world of many different types of art, opinions, films, books, TV programmes, newspapers etc. giving us a particular view of the world. It is really important that we make up our own minds about things and don't believe everything is 'real' or right.

Reflection

Ask pupils to think about a story or a TV programme they like that includes no violence.

Glossary

genre   a category or certain kind of film or book, such as comedy, romance etc.

managing anger   finding ways of controlling yourself so that you do not become violent when you are angry

media   the means of communication, such as radio and television, newspapers, and magazines, which reach or influence people widely

newsworthy   to be thought interesting enough to be covered in the news

screen media   the means of communication involving visual representation on a screen e.g. television programmes, films, computer games

screen violence   representations of violence in films, television programmes and computer games

self-defence   the right to defend yourself against attack by the use of no more force than is reasonable

tabloid   a newspaper usually characterized by an emphasis on photographs and sensational style

unacceptable   not satisfactory or not welcome

violence   the exercise of physical force, usually causing or intending to cause injuries

violent crime   crimes classed by the Home Office as robbery, sexual offences, assault and murder